EDDIE KANTAR

Classic Kantar

A COLLECTION OF BRIDGE HUMOR

MASTER POINT PRESS
Toronto

© 1999 Eddie Kantar

Master Point Press
22 Lower Village Gate
Toronto, Ontario Canada
M5P 3L7
(416) 932-9766
Internet www.pathcom.com/~raylee/

Distributed in the USA by Barricade Books
150 Fifth Avenue, Suite 700
New York, NY 10011
(800) 59-BOOKS

Canadian Cataloguing in Publication Data
Kantar, Edwin B., 1932-
Classic Kantar: a collection of bridge humor

ISBN 1-894154-14-2

1. Contract bridge — Humor I. Title

GV1282.32.K36 1999   795.41'5'0207   C99-930834-3

Editor	Ray Lee
Cover and Interior design	Olena S. Sullivan

Printed and bound in Canada
1 2 3 4 5 6 7   06 05 04 03 02 01 00 99

Foreword

by Marshall Miles

Dear Reader, you are in for a treat. I hope your spouse, if you have one, is also a bridge player — otherwise he or she may resent your putting aside all chores and remaining incommunicado for several hours while you finish the book. That's what I did, despite having seen several of the hands previously (as well as being personally involved in a few).

I played with Eddie in the days when, without modern gadgets, we never missed a slam (although the slam didn't always make). When we might bid to a game and make it while Al Roth and his partner had passed the hand out. Our specialty was getting to suit slams on a 4-3 trump fit (when lesser players, playing five-card majors, would never mention the suit we played in slam). But one time, in the Spingold, we got to 7♡. There were thirteen top tricks at notrump, but in hearts we needed a 3-3 trump split. Fortunately we got it, and I started to write plus 2210 on our score card. Eddie said, "Our captain (Ivan Erdos) is nervous about letting us play together. Let's change the contract to 7NT, plus 2220 on our score-card. It will make no difference at IMPs, and it will avoid destroying Ivan's confidence in our bidding." But our opponents overheard our conversation and tattled on us.

Eddie's stories about teaching beginners and answering bridge questions over the phone are hilarious. And when it comes to experts, not only does he have a great sense of humor, but he is prepared to name names and write about the most terrible disasters involving players of the caliber of Bob Hamman and Paul Soloway. But no one could possibly resent being placed in an unfavorable light since Eddie is always hardest of all on himself.

But enough from me. It's time to hear from the master himself.

Acknowledgments

The cartoons that are used throughout this book are by Jude Goodwin-Hansen, and originally appeared in her book *Table Talk*.

The following chapters originally appeared in *The Bridge World* and are copyright © by Bridge World Magazine Inc. :
My Father's Son, the Bridge Teacher; Short, Anyway: Panel Time; Ceci and Me; A Record, I Think; Is This Game For Real?

The following chapters originally appeared in *Bridge Today* magazine:
Long distance; Old Buddies; The In-Laws; The Book; The Cast Party; Abandon Ship; Cruising Along; Cross Ruff.

The following chapters originally appeared in the ACBL *Bulletin*:
For Eddie, it's not a Game, it's a Wild Adventure; Bridge at the Courthouse; My Home Game; Bridge Alfresco; Yvonne Makes her Little Diamond; Claim Jumper; A New Low; The Expert and the Rabbit; Drawing Trumps — an Idea Worth Some Thought.

Contents

Contents (cont.)

The Bridge Expert at Work

The Answering Service

———————— ◆ ————————

When my phone rings and I answer it with an expectant 'hello', I am secretly wishing that a soft feminine voice will be on the other end. Second choice is a close friend (any sex) and third is good news (from anyone.) Alas, what I usually get on the other end is not a hello (from either sex) but a bridge hand. And these calls can come at some very strange hours, let me assure you.

At first I was flattered that someone considered my opinion valuable enough to choose me to settle an argument. However, it soon became apparent that it wasn't my bid that was wanted, but rather, an approval of the bid that the caller had made or more likely, a display of disgust at the bid made by the caller's partner. Not only that, but the caller usually has a way of 'leaning' me towards the bid he wants to hear. For example:

Me: "Hello?"

Caller: "You hold:

♠ K J x x x   ♡ x   ◇ A Q x x   ♣ Q x x

Me (groggy): "O.K."

Caller: "You open one spade, partner bids two clubs, you bid two diamonds, partner two hearts, you three clubs, and partner four spades. You wouldn't dream of passing, would you?"

Translation — either the caller held this hand, bid, and partner got very upset, or caller's partner held the hand, passed, and a slam was missed. In any case, I know that it is right to bid on, even though I wouldn't know for sure what to do if I actually held the hand.

Me: "What, pass at this point? Surely you must be joking. Who in the world would do that?" By now, of course, the caller loves me and is glad that he woke me up. Worse, he will call again. Then of course there are the calls that don't come with any early clues about what to bid. As you are thinking about the hand, the caller becomes frantic. Maybe you will actually agree with his hated partner! Little hints start filtering in.

♠ K J x x x ♡ x ◇ A Q x x ♣ Q x x

Let's say that he has given me the hand above without any intonations, and I am thinking. Just as I am about to pass I hear, "Looks like at least a small slam, maybe even a grand if partner has the right cards, right?"

"Well," I mumble. Then finding my backbone I say, "No, I can't imagine passing. I was just thinking about the best road to either a small or a grand slam."

Then of course, there is the call from the friendly player who has just made a master bid so subtle that not even Garozzo, Belladonna and Forquet all lumped together would have thought of it. If the 'master bid' hasn't worked because partner simply couldn't cope with such a brilliancy, you are given a subtle push towards the bid, coaxing you into the same horrible quagmire. Worse, if the bid has worked, there is absolute silence on the other end as the caller is hoping (praying) you don't make the same bid so that he can describe it in all its glory. Example:

Me: "Hello?"

Caller: "You have:

♠ x x x ♡ x x ◇ A J x x x x ♣ x x

Me (groggy): "Huh?"

Caller: "Wake up! Your right hand opponent opens one club, you pass, LHO says two clubs, partner overcalls two hearts, 2NT on your right, passed around to partner who doubles. This is passed around to your LHO who retreats to three clubs and this is passed around to you. What do you do?"

WEST	NORTH	EAST	SOUTH
		1♣	pass
2♣	2♡	2NT	pass
pass	dbl	pass	pass
3♣	pass	pass	?

Silently I wait for some help. What does she want from me now? Let me review the conversation. Do the words 'retreats to three clubs' have any special significance? Is this the time for an inference double? Even I am smart enough to know that bidding diamonds (the obvious move) can't be right, or else why the call in the middle of the night? I have a few moves of my own when I need to stall for time and perhaps get an extra clue or two.

Me: "What's vulnerability?" (A very good stall!)

Caller: "Both vulnerable, what do you bid?" (I can see this is the 'brilliancy' bid and I am not going to get any further help. Nevertheless…)

Me: "Who am I playing with?"

Caller: "A very good player." (This is to let me know that they play with good partners, which is another roundabout way of telling me that they too are pretty darn good.)

Me: "Duplicate or IMPs?" (Desperation setting in.)

Caller: "Duplicate, come on."

Me: "Do we have any agreements I should know about?" (Clearly, I'm in big trouble now.)

Caller: "No, you must work it all out for yourself."

Me: "Did I play in this event? The hands look familiar." (Obviously, it's all over for me. They are going to begin the count any second.)

Caller: "No. It happened tonight."

Me: "Oh."

Caller: "So what did you bid?"

Me: "What do I bid?"

Caller: "Yes."

Me (end of my rope): "I bid 3◊."

Caller: Silence

Me (speaking faster): "What am I supposed to do, double? Does my partner have a singleton diamond or something? If he has six hearts he can correct." (Foaming.) "Don't tell me I am supposed to bid three hearts. Maybe I should just pass."

Caller: Silence.

Me (frantic): "What did you do?"

Caller (triumphantly): " I bid three notrump."

Me: "You what?"

Caller: "I bid three notrump. I was sure you would have too. Obviously partner has a strong hand with a club stopper, and he can't have too many clubs with all this club bidding on my left, so he must have some diamonds. If that is the case, I thought I could bring in three notrump. Want to know partner's hand?"

Me (crushed): "Please."

Caller (speaking louder all the time): "Partner had:

♠ A J x   ♡ A Q x x x   ◇ K 10 x   ♣ A x

I finessed the notrump bidder for Qxx of diamonds and we got a cold top."

Me: "Really, a cold top for three notrump. It looks like such an obvious contract. My partner would have bid 3NT over my 3◇."

Caller: "Oh no he wouldn't! He would have played me for a weaker diamond suit. He even told me so. Now I have another one where I made an even better bid."

Me: "Spare me. Please tell me about it tomorrow. I need a day to think about your last bid."

Caller: "O.K. Talk to me tomorrow." Click.

(Dear God, what have I ever done to deserve this?)

Long distance

There was an inevitability about the long distance call from Walter Bingham, my *Sports Illustrated* contact and very good friend. He gave me one of his 'train-bridge' problems. This time, with both sides vulnerable, sitting in the South seat I was given:

♠ J43 ♡ J96543 ◇ — ♣ 8432

WEST	NORTH	EAST	SOUTH
4◇	pass	pass	?

"What do you do?" asked Walter. I said I would pass.
"I doubled," said Walter.
"You doubled with the South hand?"
"No, silly, I doubled with the North hand,"

"Oh."

This was the entire deal:

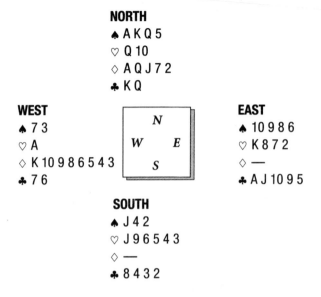

NORTH
♠ A K Q 5
♡ Q 10
◇ A Q J 7 2
♣ K Q

WEST
♠ 7 3
♡ A
◇ K 10 9 8 6 5 4 3
♣ 7 6

EAST
♠ 10 9 8 6
♡ K 8 7 2
◇ —
♣ A J 10 9 5

SOUTH
♠ J 4 2
♡ J 9 6 5 4 3
◇ —
♣ 8 4 3 2

"So how many did you set them?"

"You mean how many would we have set them if my partner had passed?"

"What happened, Walter?"

"We wound up going down four tricks doubled in five notrump. I knew I couldn't count on people like you to double if I passed, so I doubled myself."

"Good thinking, Walter."

My Father's Son, the Bridge Teacher

Early in life I decided I could either work for a living or enjoy myself. Observation had shown me that very few people could combine both. I decided to enjoy myself. I became a bridge teacher.

I have been teaching bridge for the past fifty years. I can just see Tobias Stone wincing as he reads this — he is not feeling sorry for me, mind you, but rather, for the people I've been teaching.

You see, Stoney thinks I can barely follow suit. But that's not really an insult. Stoney thinks only five people in the world play bridge, and he's not fully convinced about the other four. Incidentally, Alvin Roth and Tobias Stone have thoroughly indoctrinated their followers that five-card majors are the only way to play. If I ever happen to get a decent result against a Roth-Stoner by opening a four-card major, he invariably takes my hand out of the board and he and his partner examine my four-card suit as though it were some kind of snake.

However, for all of Stone's conversations, Roth makes him look like a piker. In Toronto, when Marshall Miles and I played (and I use the term generously) on the same K.O. team with them, Roth would inspire confidence in Marshall and me by making a plane reservation home before each match. I only mention this because I used to teach my classes to open four-card majors, if the hand called for it, and I wanted the five-card majorites to know this before reading on. Four-card-major propaganda may be on their banned reading list.

Oh yes, I also used to teach them to count for long suits instead of short ones when originally evaluating their hands. I would estimate conservatively that this has cost me close to three years of my life in futile explanations. I now teach them to wait until a fit has been uncovered before counting points for short suits. Early in my 'career' I mentioned that in order to give your partner a double raise you need at least four trumps and 13-16 points in support of partner's suit. Suddenly a woman began leafing through her Goren Book. She looked at the woman she came with, and with obvious relief, said, "He's going to be all right — he tells the truth!" Now that I am in my declining years I have recklessly begun to teach limit raises. Live it up, and let the chips fall where they may.

I started out naively enough, by teaching beginners. I should have realized immediately that I was not cut out for this. In one of my first classes I walked over to help someone play a hand. After a few tricks every single card in the dummy was good and there was no way, even for this lady, to lose another trick. I simply said, "Go over to the dummy and take the rest of the tricks." With that, I left to assist at another table. As I glanced back I saw the lady walking around the table to get over to the dummy!

At times they call me over to the table. "What should I play now?" the declarer usually asks me.

I take a look and see six cards in everybody's hand. "What's trump?" I ask, stalling for time.

"Hearts."

"Do they have any left?"

"One or two, but only little ones."

"Are those clubs in dummy good?"

"I don't remember, it's been a long time since they were played. Esther," she asks her right-hand opponent, "are those clubs in dummy good?"

"How should I know? I'm not playing the hand."

By this time, I've taken a peek at all of the hands. You would never believe some of the endings!

Sometimes they come and tell me about a hand they played at home the night before. "I was playing with my husband," the story usually begins (she's clearly looking for sympathy, but she forgets I'm on his side), "and he bid three spades. What should I have done?"

"You mean he opened three spades?"

"No, I bid one heart, he gave me one spade, I gave him three clubs," (this is a very generous game) "and he mentioned three spades. What should I have done?"

"Do you remember your hand?" I try.

"Oh yes, my hand. I had no spades — or maybe one — the queen, king, ten, ace, nine and an 'x' in hearts — like you put on the board — the king of diamonds with some others, and the rest clubs, but it doesn't matter. Anyway, I said four hearts and he said we could have made three notrump. Was he right?"

"No," I say, hating myself, "you were right. You had an automatic four heart bid."

The last straw came up a few years ago when I was teaching the fifth lesson of a series for beginners. One particular lady came to class thinking it was the first lesson, and she just happened to sit South. I had a prepared hand on the table, open-faced, and was about to explain the bidding. I began by saying that South was the dealer and that with fourteen points and a five-card spade suit — in beginning classes you give them at least five-card suits or they won't bid at all — the correct opening was one spade.

"Mr. Kantar," this woman said, raising her hand, "which spade should I bid?"

After a bit you get to recognize questions of this type. If you try to answer them you usually wind up wishing you had gone to work for a living. I parried.

"Why don't you wait a bit and you'll see what the bidding means?" She seemed satisfied, so I continued.

"South opens one spade…"

"Mr. Kantar, where should I put the spade that South opens?"

Well, I answered that question, and that is why I no longer teach 'beginning' classes. I now call my classes 'intermediate' and 'advanced'. I find the fact that the same people come does not disturb me.

In all of these classes I start out by giving a short lecture on the topic of the day and then call out prepared hands for distribution at the tables. Each player takes a suit, and I call off one suit at a time. Using this method I can teach any number of tables without trouble

— provided everyone distributes the cards properly.

The fact that 'eight' and 'ace' sound so much alike has caused endless confusion — to say nothing of those students who forget to distribute the suit they are holding; to say nothing of the fact that somebody always winds up with too many or too few cards; to say nothing of the fact that almost no one bothers to count his cards; to say nothing of my mistakes as I call the cards. Otherwise, it is an infallible system.

In one of my 'beginning' classes (which I had been teaching for about five years) on preemptive bidding, a truly memorable event occurred. Having called out the hands, I noticed that one lady had wound up with twenty cards (her partner's seven-card suit) and her partner only six! True to their code of trusting me implicitly, it didn't seem to faze either of them.

The lady with the twenty cards was one of my better students; by that I mean she had decided to go all out and count for long suits, regardless of what certain books said. She was trying to count up her hand, but her real problem was in trying to hold on to her cards. She needed a basket; they kept falling. Finally she got organized, and with her 6-8-4-2 distribution she came through admirably with a one heart opening. Next hand passed, and her partner was in a quandary.

This was an older woman, who had counted points for short suits all her life, and she wasn't going to let a young upstart change her bidding habits. Relying on her years of experience, she realized that with her 0-1-3-2 distribution she had a truly magnificent hand. Why, in short suits alone she practically had an opening bid! Finally she called me over.

"Mr. Kantar, Mr. Kantar!" she shouted hysterically. "I've never seen a hand like this before! What should I bid?"

Had I been in a particularly fiendish mood I would have counted up her hand with her, but the sight of her partner trying valiantly to hold her cards sobered me and I finally revealed all. But it hurt.

Some students have been so overcome with my teaching that they can't wait to tell me how much they got out of a lesson. A little while back a lady came up to me after class and said that the lesson

I had given the week before on redoubles had really helped her. She proceeded to tell me about a recent hand.

"My right-hand opponent opened one heart and I doubled. Next player passed, and my partner redoubled — just as you said, because she had more than ten points."

"Redoubled?" I said. "Your partner can't redouble your double."

"Oh," she said, "I knew there was something funny about that bidding."

Over the years, one tries not to repeat the same mistakes. The error I keep making is trying to teach them which card to lead, especially in partner's suit. I know and they know that they are going to lead the highest card, no matter what I say, but they are very polite while I'm explaining. One lady, however, couldn't stand it.

As I was going through my spiel of why it is better to lead low from an honor, this woman stood up in the middle of the room and said, "I can't. They won't let me do it at my Women's Club. I have to lead my highest."

So what are you going to do about that?

If there is one thing a dedicated teacher likes to see it is progress. A clear indication of lesson application was hammered home to me after a class on card-combinations which included 'Surrounding Plays'.

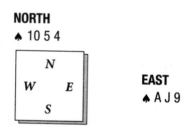

NORTH
♠ 10 5 4

EAST
♠ A J 9

East is on lead, and having the ten in dummy 'surrounded' with the J-9 should lead the jack. This seemed simple enough. I had concocted a hand where East would eventually get the lead, and with a K-J-9 over a ten in dummy, was to lead with the jack. However, I overlooked something. At Trick 1, West led a small card in a different suit, and this was the dummy's holding in the suit led:

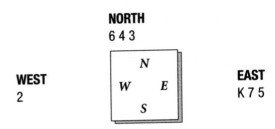

NORTH
6 4 3

WEST
2

EAST
K 7 5

Dummy played low and East played the seven, thereby triumphantly 'surrounding' the six-spot! I later analyzed the play and decided the conflict between third-hand-high and the 'surrounding' lesson was just too much. East had cracked under the pressure.

Incidentally, third-hand play is one of my favorite lessons because it gives me a chance to ask questions like this:

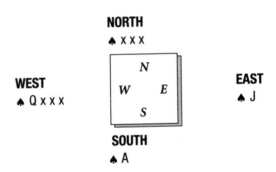

NORTH
♠ X X X

WEST
♠ Q x x x

EAST
♠ J

SOUTH
♠ A

I ask them (after sufficient explanation) to pretend that they are West, defending a notrump contract.

"Assume," I say, "you lead a low card and your partner plays the jack, which loses to declarer's ace. Who has the king?" (That, of course, is a pretty tough one for the class, but I am ruthless.)

Aside from the few who think it is in the dummy, most of the people who believe that falsecarding amounts to cheating will answer 'East'. The bright ones always say 'South' but I once had a lady who liked to play safe. Her answer was 'Southeast.'

In line with this scheme, I was trying to get the point across of unblocking for your partner in situations like this:

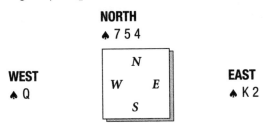

NORTH
♠ 7 5 4

WEST
♠ Q

EAST
♠ K 2

I said, "Pretend you are East and that your partner leads the queen of spades against notrump. Which card would you play?" Silence. "Come on," I urged, "take a chance."

Finally one brave soul said that she would play the king.

"Really?" I teased. "Would you actually put your king on partner's queen?"

"No," she finally admitted, "I wouldn't, but I think you would — you're so tricky!"

As I mentioned earlier, I enjoy my work, and I even teach a few people to play. Take the lady who, as declarer, would never attack a suit in which she didn't have the ace and king. Finally I forced her (by wrenching the card from her hand) to lead up to a king-jack combination in dummy. I carefully explained that it was simply a guess — if she thought the ace was on her left she should play the king, and if she thought it was on her right, she should play the jack. I went through it again, then asked her which one she wanted to play from dummy, and to tell me what she was hoping for when she made her play. After indescribable agony, she finally played the king.

"What are you hoping for?" I asked.

"I'm hoping they make a mistake."

Tales Out of School

It has been estimated that there are in the vicinity of 17,000,000 bridge players in the United States. To the novice player that figure seems somewhat high but reasonable. The average player doesn't really believe it; the expert player knows in his heart that there are no more than ten bridge players in all the land, while the bridge teacher wonders if there is even one.

The teacher of beginning and intermediate bridge classes is doomed to a life of frustration. Most of his students simply will not play between lessons and those who do are subjected to so much advice from their friends who are 'expert' players that they seldom, if ever, recover from this compendium of misinformation.

Let's start with a few of my own experiences from beginning classes, which I no longer teach. The reason that I stopped teaching beginners is that I was afraid I would forget how to play myself if I continued. Their logic is so illogical that sooner or later I begin to fall victim to it. To wit: in all my classes I have the students distribute the cards. Each one starts with an entire suit and I instruct them, one suit at a time, how to divide the cards. After five lessons of this type of distribution one lady who had yet to distribute the diamonds suddenly thought she had been dealt thirteen of them! In the middle of the class she jumped up and screamed, "Alice, you wouldn't believe this hand!"

Then there was the lady who went wild over singletons. On one hand she was dealt twelve cards including a singleton spade. She called me over to help her straighten out the hand. I found the missing card on the floor, it was the ace of spades. As I placed it in her hand she told me, "Now you've gone and wrecked my hand."

I've learned, after many bitter years, that most players simply do not know their directions. Nowadays I place directional guide cards

on the table and point North at the blackboard. I do this because I chalk up the hand that they are playing and it becomes somewhat easier for them to orient themselves. What I mean is, it should be easier. I have one group in Pasadena who simply will not play unless North is placed the same way that it is in Pasadena.

Then this happened to me. I occasionally teach private lessons at home. This particular group of four ladies was very eager to brush up on their game because they hadn't played for a long time. So I went to one of their homes and as each of the 'girls' came in, there was much said about beauty parlors, dresses, divorces, marriages, etc. On the first hand one lady after sorting her cards started placing some threes face up on the table. I asked her what she was doing. "Oh, she replied, I thought we were playing canasta."

A few months later in yet another beginning class, I found out how cruel a person I really was. Declarer was playing the hand in spades. In dummy was the ◇AJ5 and in her own hand, the singleton deuce. The opening lead was the king of diamonds which declarer captured with the ace. Later in the hand, the opening leader tried to cash the queen of diamonds which declarer ruffed. As I was leaving the table for a few seconds I saw that declarer was correctly drawing trumps. Upon returning I found that everyone was discussing something or other. I casually asked declarer if the jack of diamonds in the dummy was a good trick or not. She looked up at me and said, "We were just talking over spades, and now you ask about diamonds. What are you, a sadist or something?"

For some reason whenever I give an illustration of how a particular suit should be played by the defenders, I make the suit spades. In this case I was showing when the queen should be played from the queen jack (usually when partner leads the king). After the class was over one fellow came up to me and asked me to settle a bet. His wife had bet him that the only suit in which you should drop the queen from the queen-jack is spades. Beautiful.

Then there was the lady who was playing a notrump contract with the ♡AKQ2 on the table and the ♡J43 in her own hand. At one point she had to make a discard from the table and she wanted to discard the deuce of hearts even though she needed four tricks from that suit to make her contract. As she was reaching for the deuce of hearts, a slightly over-emotional "No!" came from me. This naturally caused her to drop all of her cards face up on the table. After we retrieved them, I pointed out that by careful play — placing the jack on the deuce — this suit could actually be brought in for four tricks. She shook her head disgustedly. "I missed that key play, didn't I?" As I was leaving the table I heard one opponent say to the other— "Do you think we'll ever be able to see things like that?"

Then there is the group who, no matter how many mistakes they make, tell themselves that they are coming to class just to pass time, and that they really know everything that I'm telling them. Some of the reasons that I have heard for their mistakes are:

1. I can't play when he is watching.
2. They're all trick hands anyway.
3. I wouldn't bid, play, defend(choose any three) that way if it wasn't a lesson.
4. Too much pressure around here.
5. I have better partners when I play at home.
6. We're just not trying.
7. Oh, he thinks he's so smart with those key plays of his.

Then there are the superstitious ones. "I don't bid slams, they never make." "I don't like hands with four aces." "I never finesse with eight cards missing the queen, I don't care what the rule says." Also from the same lady, "The player who holds the nine always has the queen, I don't care."

Once I was called to fill in for a hand. I was the dealer and these were the two hands:

OPENER (Me)		RESPONDER (She)
♠ 10 4	N	♠ A K J 5
♡ A Q 9 7 6	W E	♡ J 10 3
◊ Q 10 4	S	◊ A K
♣ A 7 6		♣ K 10 8 5

Our advanced bidding went like this:

ME	SHE
1♡	4NT
5♡	6♡
pass	

Me to she: "Why did you jump to 4NT so quickly? I might have had a four-card heart suit." (We were playing four-card majors.)

She to me: "What do you mean? You rebid them, didn't you?"

Then there was the advanced, advanced lesson on endplays. As I came over to one table I asked the declarer, a particularly pretty young thing, if she had played for the endplay.

"No," she replied, "I decided to play for a revoke instead."

"And how did you do that?" I asked naively.

"Oh," she answered, "I switched suits every trick."

Then there were the rabble rousers. All my classes know by now that I will open a strong four-card major and that I avoid opening three-card club suits if possible. Merely by admitting that, I have alienated myself more than if I had admitted to being a communist.

This one man brought up this hand written on a piece of paper:

♠ A K J 10   ♡ K J 10   ◇ Q 5 4   ♣ 10 9 4

and asked me what I would open. Before anything, I told him, "You know I avoid opening a short club." He said he did too, he would much rather open with a short diamond!

One week I gave a lesson on the Stayman convention and the following week I was watching a player who held:

♠ A 10 5 4   ♡ K Q 8 7   ◇ 6 5 4   ♣ 6 5

Her right hand opponent opened 1◇ and she overcalled, naturally, with 2♣.

"What are you doing?" I asked.

"Oh, I was making a Stayman," she replied.

Then there was the cagey declarer. In 7NT the last three cards around the table were:

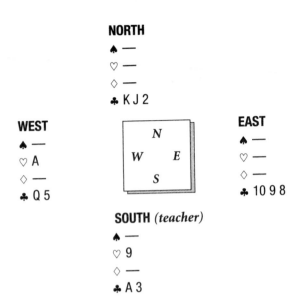

NORTH
♠ —
♡ —
◇ —
♣ K J 2

WEST
♠ —
♡ A
◇ —
♣ Q 5

N
W   E
S

EAST
♠ —
♡ —
◇ —
♣ 10 9 8

SOUTH *(teacher)*
♠ —
♡ 9
◇ —
♣ A 3

Declarer had yet to lose a trick and the lead was in his own hand. Things look pretty good, right? Wrong. Declarer led a low club to the king and then a low club back to the ace, even though he knew his nine of hearts was not high, and eventually conceded a trick to the ace of that suit. As this play was made by a very intelligent person, I couldn't resist asking him what was going through his mind.

SOMETIMES ONE JUST HAS TO BREAK THE RULES IN ORDER TO BE BRILLIANT

It turned out that he originally had the queen of hearts in his hand but he had discarded it for deceptive purposes, retaining the nine. In the end he confessed that he had been so impressed with his own discard that he wanted to see if he had fooled anyone.

Sometimes I am overcome with feelings of guilt and I can't help but warn them about the traps I have set for them. For example:

Vul: Both
Dealer: West

NORTH
♠ 7 4
♡ A K 5
◇ A K 10 9 8 7
♣ A 2

WEST
♠ A Q 9 3 2
♡ J 10 7 6
◇ 2
♣ K Q 10

EAST
♠ 10 8 5
♡ 9 8
◇ J 5 4 3
♣ 8 7 6 5

SOUTH
♠ K J 6
♡ Q 4 3 2
◇ Q 6
♣ J 9 4 3

WEST	NORTH	EAST	SOUTH
1♠	dbl	pass	2♡
pass	3◇	pass	3NT
all pass			

Opening Lead: ♠3

The gist of the hand is for South to win the spade opening, cross to a high heart and run the ten of diamonds. This is a safety play to guard against East having four diamonds to the jack and being able to punch a spade through South's king. From bitter experience I know that this hand is a bit much for an intermediate class, so I warned them to be careful of the diamond suit.

One lady took my warning so much to heart that she won the spade opening and played the ace and a low club ducking the trick to West's queen. Now it was easy for her to establish her ninth trick in clubs without monkeying with diamonds at all!

Then of course, there are the sleepers. This I don't mind as long

as they don't snore. They are invariably husbands who have been literally dragged along by their wives to learn the 'finer points'.

Some of the sleepers will take an occasional nap but this one fellow falls soundly asleep the minute I open my mouth. During the
lesson on third-hand play I always throw in this hand:

Vul: Both
Dealer: North

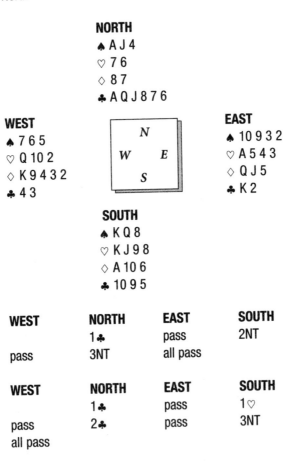

NORTH
♠ A J 4
♡ 7 6
◇ 8 7
♣ A Q J 8 7 6

WEST
♠ 7 6 5
♡ Q 10 2
◇ K 9 4 3 2
♣ 4 3

EAST
♠ 10 9 3 2
♡ A 5 4 3
◇ Q J 5
♣ K 2

SOUTH
♠ K Q 8
♡ K J 9 8
◇ A 10 6
♣ 10 9 5

WEST	NORTH	EAST	SOUTH
	1♣	pass	2NT
pass	3NT	all pass	

WEST	NORTH	EAST	SOUTH
	1♣	pass	1♡
pass	2♣	pass	3NT
all pass			

Opening Lead: ◇ 3

I have learned always to put at least two bidding sequences on
the board for each hand. If I don't someone will always ask if they

can't bid the hand another way. In any case, I have explained at length before the hand is distributed that third hand should play the lower or lowest of touching honors when partner leads a small card and dummy also has small cards.

On the actual hand I had simply wanted East to play the jack, then the queen, and finally a low diamond to South's ace. When South eventually finesses clubs, East is supposed to lead a *low* heart trying to put West in to run the diamonds. South is supposed to go up with the king because the hand cannot be made if West has the ace of hearts, so South might as well play East for that card.

Yes, I know that this hand can be beaten if, after winning the first two diamonds, East shifts to a low heart immediately. The defense must then come to two diamonds, two hearts and a club. However, this defense has never been found until… until my sleeper picked up the East cards.

This was his defense, never having heard a word of the lesson, naturally. At Trick 1 he played the queen of diamonds, of course. When South ducked he returned a *low heart*. Now South finessed the jack and West won the queen and played a low diamond! The fact that South must have the ace and jack of diamonds never bothered her. When East put up the jack of diamonds, South was forced to duck again. My sleeper continued with another low heart and when declarer finessed the nine West won the ten and the hand was defeated two tricks while at most other tables the hand was being made. What should I say? And what difference would it make. He was already sleeping.

Then of course, we deal with the most common type of all — the nervous player. She is afraid that every time she breathes she is making a mistake. The nervous player tends to become very emotional if, for example, something exciting like a finesse works. Recently this combination of cards arose in a lesson hand:

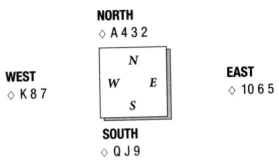

NORTH

◇ A 4 3 2

WEST

◇ K 8 7

EAST

◇ 10 6 5

SOUTH

◇ Q J 9

This was the lesson on second hand play and the idea was for West not to cover the queen of diamonds from the closed hand because it might expose East's ten to a finesse if declarer had QJ9. I might add at this point, that in all my years of teaching, only three West players have *not* covered the queen, so indoctrinated are they to cover an honor with an honor.

Anyway, at this table the queen was covered, naturally, and declarer in a moment of monumental inspiration won the ace, finessed the nine on the way back, cashed the jack and set up the four of diamonds for the contract-making discard. Feeling safe that declarer would use the four of diamonds to discard her obvious loser, I made my usual error of leaving the table prematurely. Upon returning, I saw the four of diamonds on the table and the opponents taking the setting trick because declarer had neglected to use the card.

I finally asked her what she did with her last diamond. She pointed to it and said, "It's right there, I was too excited to do anything with it."

Then there is one table of women that I will never forget. I know secretly why they come to my classes — to torment each other. They have no greater pleasure than to see a mistake being made, even if by their own partner. It would all be fairly humorous if they would only keep quiet once in a while. There is no way I can get a word in edgewise to the class until they are through chewing each other out. Rather than get angry I decided to listen to what they were saying to one another. This is the way it usually went:

"Let me alone, I didn't lead the deuce, you did."

"I did not, I didn't even have the deuce. You know what he says about deuces anyway."

"I don't care what he says about deuces, you led one, so let me alone."

"Shhh, he's going to explain, let's listen and see who had the deuce and you let me alone."

Among the most dangerous of all students are the 'rule memorizers' and the 'convention experts'.

My 'rule experts' always lead trumps because they are forever 'in doubt'. They never lead away from a king because it is a gigantic no-no. They lead through strength even if that strength consists of AKQJx and they still lead the highest card in their partner's suit because their great-grandmother did. Those, of course, are the old-fashioned 'rule experts'. The modern variety offer something new and dashing to the scene.

In one lesson I was trying to help them read the opponents' leads. I mentioned that if a deuce was led, particularly at notrump, the opening leader would have a four-card suit and it would therefore be simple for declarer to work out how many cards the leader's partner held.

I made a particular point of mentioning the value of keeping an eye on the small cards because if the opening leader is leading his smallest card he usually has led from a four-card suit. Therefore, if the four is led and the three and deuce are visible the opening leader likely had a four-card suit, whereas if either the three or the deuce is invisible the opening leader could have a five-card suit if he has the missing card.

From the back of the room. "Does this mean the Rule of Eleven doesn't work anymore?"

Now for a word from our conventions expert. Once again I was explaining when an honor should be covered and when it shouldn't. (I am so convincing when I give this lecture that I almost forget how many mistakes I have made in this same situation.) We were going over the typical situation where the student is West:

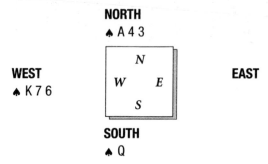

NORTH
♠ A 4 3

WEST
♠ K 7 6

EAST

SOUTH
♠ Q

I mentioned that if a decent South player leads the queen, the presumption is that the closed hand contains the jack as well. And, if we could *see* both the queen and the jack, we would cover the second honor; so we should wait for the jack to be led. "But what if they are playing Rusinow leads?" someone blurts out.

Nor can we overlook a species known the world over — 'the mad signaler' and his country cousin 'the random discarder'. It is literally 1000 to 1 that if one of these players makes either a signal or a discard it will cost an average of 1.563 tricks per deal.

In order to help out these poor misguided souls I have given them a few rules to follow, especially if I ever play with them professionally. I have one particular fellow in mind whose signaling and discarding were what you might term mildly 'far out'. I told him that I would prefer he didn't signal me at all as I usually could tell what was going on anyway. (The translation of this is — after the hand is over I always know what I should have done.)

And as for discarding:

1. Always keep the same length as dummy.
2. Do not discard down to a void.
3. Do not discard from a suit declarer has bid, or at least try and keep the same number of cards that you think declarer has in the suit.
4. As a general rule, discard from a suit you do not want led so you can preserve length and strength in the suit or suits you do want led.

With this as background you can imagine the torment he must have been going through during the defense of the following hand:

Vul: Neither
Dealer: North

<pre>
                    NORTH
                    ♠ K J 10 9 8
                    ♡ A K 8 3
                    ◇ 7 6
                    ♣ 8 5

WEST   EAST (teacher)
♠ Q 7 6 5 4   ┌─────────┐   ♠ A 3 2
♡ 10   │   N   │   ♡ Q 9 7 5 2
◇ Q 8 5 4 3 2   │ W   E │   ◇ J 9
♣ 7   │   S   │   ♣ K 6 3
                   └─────────┘
                    SOUTH
                    ♠ —
                    ♡ J 6 4
                    ◇ A K 10
                    ♣ A Q J 10 9 4 2
</pre>

Against weak opponents, the bidding went:

WEST	NORTH	EAST	SOUTH
	1♠	pass	2♣
pass	2♡	pass	3◇
pass	3♠	pass	3NT
all pass			

My boy decided to lead the ten of hearts, which was ducked to my queen. Having a perfect picture of the whole hand I decided to return a heart to kill dummy's entry to the spade suit. (On target, as usual.) Anyway, I led back a heart and when declarer played the jack I think I actually saw perspiration on my partner's forehead. You see, he had to make a discard, and every discard would violate a rule! A spade was out because he had to keep the same length as dummy; a diamond was out because declarer had bid that suit and he had to keep as many as declarer! A club was out because he was not supposed to void himself in any suit.

After much soul-searching he finally discarded the seven of

clubs. Declarer, who tended to take everything at face value, decided my partner had the king of clubs and that it was fruitless to take the finesse. After all, a seven is a seven is a seven

Finally declarer played the ace and queen of clubs to my king. Don't ask what torture my partner underwent during these two plays. I finally cashed my ace of spades to hold the hand to four notrump for a clear top.

My other good board playing professionally still sticks with me.

NORTH
♠ K 4
♡ K 10 2
◇ K 10 9 8 7
♣ 7 6 5

WEST (Me)
♠ 9 8 7 6 5
♡ 3
◇ J 6 5
♣ A 4 3 2

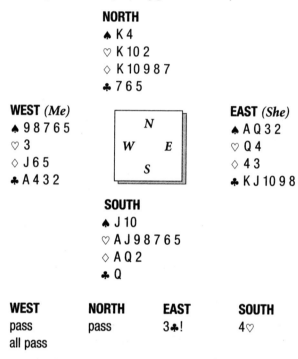

EAST (She)
♠ A Q 3 2
♡ Q 4
◇ 4 3
♣ K J 10 9 8

SOUTH
♠ J 10
♡ A J 9 8 7 6 5
◇ A Q 2
♣ Q

WEST	NORTH	EAST	SOUTH
pass	pass	3♣!	4♡
all pass			

Opening Lead: ♣A

Although it is true that we can make four spades, nobody was in it and four hearts was making at every table — except ours. We beat it! After scoring my ace of clubs I shifted to a spade at Trick 2. My partner scored two spade tricks and returned the king of clubs. Declarer, fearing a singleton club in my hand, ruffed with the ace of hearts and my partner's queen of trumps became the setting trick.

Bridge is a lovely game, I love to teach it, and in my other world of expert players, I don't have nearly as much fun.

Old Buddies

The phone rings. It's an old table tennis buddy of mine, Herb, who belongs to a country club where I have taught several series of bridge lessons. Herb and his wife, Frances, both prominent lawyers, are into bridge and attend my classes. It turns out that Herb has two friends, a husband and wife, visiting from Haifa, Israel. They too are bridge players and own several of my books. Would I please, please be his guest for dinner one evening and then play just one hour of bridge with his friends? They like my books and he is sure that it would be a great treat for them.

We wind up at this fabulous Italian *ristorante* and gorge ourselves like you wouldn't believe. It turns out that the couple from Israel was born in Rumania and emigrated to Israel about seventeen years ago. They even own a bridge book that my cousin Nicu wrote. They also tell me that they are Precision players but that most Israelis play Acol. I find out that there are about five to six thousand tournament players in Israel, including many juniors. Given the size of the country, this is an impressive figure.

We adjourn to Herb's home. Conveniently, there are eight of us. He suggests that I play with him against the Israeli couple while the others watch. I suggest that perhaps the others would rather play. It is agreed we will play a two-rubber bridge game. We decide to play Chicago. The first three hands are uneventful. On the fourth deal I pick up:

♠ 9 6 4 3   ♡ A Q 7 2   ◇ 5 4   ♣ A J 7

Herb opens one diamond and the next hand doubles. I redouble. It proceeds two clubs to my left, passed back to me. I try two notrump and this is raised to three notrump. The husband, to my left, asks me about the one diamond opening bid. I tell him I think my partner really has diamonds. In the meantime, Herb has vanished into the other room to tell the other players that I am about to play a hand. Maybe they would like to watch. Grudgingly, they trudge in.

The opening lead is the ◇Q, and this is what I see:

Vul: Both sides bloated
Dealer: North

NORTH
♠ K 8
♡ 8 3
◇ A K 10 9 8 7 6
♣ 3 2

Lead: ◇ Q

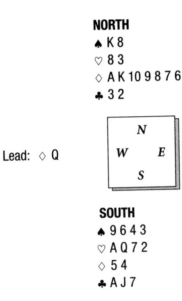

SOUTH
♠ 9 6 4 3
♡ A Q 7 2
◇ 5 4
♣ A J 7

Well, have you decided what you would do with this lead? As I agonize, my kibitzers check the diamond holdings in the East-West hands. Great. Herb, who paid a fortune for this dinner, is eagerly waiting for me to 'shine'. After all, in class I always know what to bid and play. (I should — I make up the hands.)

Well, I can't sit here forever. I am supposed to be the 'expert'. Finally, I decide to duck the opening lead — East follows. Then comes a low spade. I play low from dummy and East wins the queen and then cashes the ace. I can just see East cashing two more spades while the diamonds were all good originally. No, East starts to think. Good, the spades must be blocked. East returns the ♣K. I win and lead a diamond to the ace. East follows with the jack. Diamonds were 2-2 all along. Looks pass among kibitzers.

I run the diamonds and eventually take the heart finesse. You didn't think that was going to work, did you? No, of course not. West started with:

♠ J 5 2   ♡ K 9 5   ♢ Q 2   ♣ 9 8 6 5 4

Down one. Silence. For this he fed me and brought me to his home? Oh well, two fewer students at my next class, if I ever teach at Herb's country club again. However, that's still better than winning the opening lead, crossing to the ♡A and finessing the ♢10 — down five! Once word of that got out, I wouldn't have any students in *any* of my classes.

The In-Laws

Talk about pressure. A friend of mind and her boyfriend invited me over the other evening. She was entertaining her daughter's in-laws. This couple had taken lessons from me many years ago so there was method to her madness. Despite fearing what I might be letting myself in for, I accepted nonetheless (a dinner is a dinner). After the dinner the 'game' started. I could see that great things were expected of me, the teacher.

I wound up playing with the mother-in-law. The 'boyfriend', a beginner, was on my right and the father-in-law (don't ask) on my left. First hand out of the box I found myself gazing at:

♠ A Q J 9 8 6 4 2   ♡ A 3   ◇ K 10   ♣ 5

The boyfriend dealt and opened one club. My four-spade overcall ended the auction. This is what I saw:

NORTH *(expectant mother-in-law —*
♠ 10 3   *expecting me to make it)*
♡ Q 7 4
◇ 8 7 6 4
♣ K 7 6 4

Lead: ♣8

```
      N
  W       E
      S
```

SOUTH *(teacher)*
♠ A Q J 9 8 6 4 2
♡ A 3
◇ K 10
♣ 5

I ducked to East's queen and East continued with the ♣A which I ruffed. West playing the ♣J, a likely honest card. Given the extraordinary level of the game, how should I continue?

Calling on all my bridge smarts, I cleverly exited with the ♠8 to East's king. East continued with a club, which I ruffed high. I entered dummy with a spade, discarded a heart on the ♣K and confidently led up to the ◇K. Down one. The father-in-law's hand:

♠ 7 5   ♡ K 10 8 5   ◇ A Q 9 5 2   ♣ J 8

Nobody doubles the teacher.
The boyfriend had:

♠ K   ♡ J 9 6 2   ◇ J 3   ♣ A Q 10 9 3 2

Of course, if West leads the ♣J and continues the suit, I will be compelled to plunk down the ♠A. When the king falls, I can play ace and a heart making the hand whenever West has the ♡K or East the ◇A. Well, maybe they didn't notice. Then the dreaded words from East: "Gee, I had a singleton king of spades and I made a trick with it. Did you pull the wrong card, Eddie?"

"Yes," I say. "I meant to lead the ♠9." This pathetic attempt at humor slides right by the table, of course. Two hands later I pick up:

♠ 10 4   ♡ Q 6 4   ◇ Q 10 9 6 3   ♣ K 10 9

My partner opens an artificial two clubs and teacher responds two diamonds. When partner rebids two notrump, I give a cheery three notrump. Oops, a bit too cheery. Partner now tortures me by rebidding four notrump (I knew the dinner wouldn't be worth this). As I am squirming over this new turn of events, the boyfriend informs me that four notrump sounds like Blackwood to him. Thanks. Forsaking this expert advice, and beginning to sweat a bit, I pass. This is the hand:

I KNEW IT!
I KNEW NO MATTER WHAT I DID HE'D YELL

NORTH *(mildly sweating teacher)*
- ♠ 10 4
- ♡ Q 6 4
- ◇ Q 10 9 6 3
- ♣ K 10 9

WEST *(boyfriend)*
- ♠ J 8 6 2
- ♡ 10 7
- ◇ 8 7
- ♣ J 8 7 6 4

```
        N
   W         E
        S
```

EAST *(father-in-law)*
- ♠ K 7 5 3
- ♡ A 9 5 3 2
- ◇ 5 2
- ♣ Q 3

SOUTH *(mother-in-law)*
- ♠ A Q 9
- ♡ K J 8
- ◇ A K J 4
- ♣ A 5 2

West leads the ♣6 and dummy's nine fetches the queen and ace. At this point I take a peek into their hands hoping against hope that we haven't missed a laydown slam. I catch a glimpse of an ace to my left, so at least we haven't a grand. However, there is bad news. With the club and the spade finesses both working there are twelve tricks. But will she be able to take them? I find myself rooting against my partner! Maybe she won't realize she has three club tricks available.

Anyway, I am heartened by her first play: a diamond to the queen, blocking that suit. Next comes a heart to the jack followed by the ♡K. East winds and returns a spade. She pauses. Please, God, anything but the queen. Queen. More bad news: She unblocks the diamonds and crosses to the ♡Q to cash the fifth diamond, discarding a club. With a heavy heart I notices that this is the three-card ending:

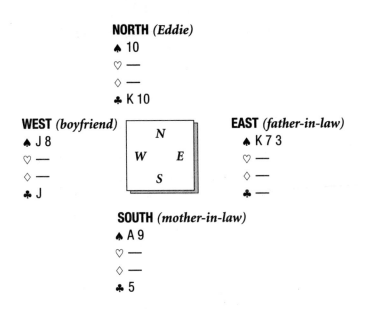

NORTH *(Eddie)*
♠ 10
♡ —
◇ —
♣ K 10

WEST *(boyfriend)*
♠ J 8
♡ —
◇ —
♣ J

EAST *(father-in-law)*
♠ K 7 3
♡ —
◇ —
♣ —

SOUTH *(mother-in-law)*
♠ A 9
♡ —
◇ —
♣ 5

When West blanks the ♣J to guard spades, my last hope is gone. Now the mother-in-law cashes the ♣K (believe me, she doesn't know there is only one club out) but wonder of wonders, she doesn't know the ♣10 is high. Mercifully she enters her hand with a spade and gives up the last trick.

"Nice pass," she says.

"Nicely played," I hear myself saying.

Bridge in the fast lane.

Many years ago I kibitzed Roger Stern and Larry Rosler playing in the Spingold. After a rather complicated sequence, Roger asked for aces using their own response schedule. After the 'systemic' response, Roger bid seven of the agreed suit. The opening lead was made and Roger took one look at the dummy and said, "Larry, this is the end of the world." (An ace was missing.)

So what does that have to do with this chapter? Some time ago I completed a book entitled *Take Your Tricks*. This is a book of 557 tips on the play of the hand. Tip 120 in the section 'Notrump Play' says: with two stoppers (in the suit that has been led) and two cards to remove, you may be able to control which entry to remove first. Attack the entry, or the possible entry, of the player with the greater length in the suit that has been led. Here is the example that went along with the tip:

NORTH *(Dummy)*
♠ 4 3
♡ 10 6 5 4
◊ Q J 10 5
♣ A K 4

WEST
♠ Q J 10 9 8
♡ 8 7
◊ K 8 7
♣ J 3 2

```
      N
   W     E
      S
```

EAST
♠ 6 5 2
♡ A 9 3 2
◊ 6 4
♣ 10 9 8 7

SOUTH *(You)*
♠ A K 7
♡ K Q J
◊ A 9 3 2
♣ Q 6 5

The analysis went on to say that you should win the second spade, cross to a club and take the diamond finesse, trying first to knock out the entry of the player with the likely spade length. Later when you knock out the ♡A, East will be spadeless and you will have made your contract.

The problem is that you have nine top tricks by simply knocking out the ♡A! Finessing diamonds early is the only way to go down! What happened was a typo — the ♡10 was not supposed to be in the dummy, dummy was supposed to have four small hearts. Thank God the name of the book was not *Count Your Tricks*.

When I got the first of three letters referring to this, I said to myself, "Eddie, this is the end of the world." But it wasn't. I got another letter saying that Tip 164 contained 'a major analytical stupidity!' The tip itself was harmless enough. It stated: a finesse in one suit is more likely than a 3-3 break in another suit. Once again it was the example that was the problem. This was the hand that I used:

NORTH (*Dummy*)
♠ A Q
♡ 5 4 3
◇ A 7 6 5
♣ 5 4 3 2

SOUTH (*You*)
♠ 8 7 2
♡ J 9 6
◇ K Q 3
♣ A K Q J

Playing three notrump, West leads a low heart from ♡K10xx and the opponents cash four heart tricks. At Trick 5 West shifts to a spade. Should you finesse? According to the tip you should, because the spade finesse (50%) is a better chance than a 3-3 diamond division (36%). These figures apply with a spade opening lead, but now that the opponents have cashed four hearts there are squeeze possibilities. I was told that it is now 2% better to go up with the ♠A and play for a squeeze on West (if he happens to have four or more diamonds along with the ♠K) or a squeeze on East if he happens to have four or more diamonds along with the ♠KJ109.

I consulted with my own mathematician-in-waiting and he said it was 1% better to take the finesse, because West started with more hearts and was therefore slightly less likely to have four or more diamonds. Also, if West had four or more diamonds, given the missing spot cards, he might have led from a diamond sequence. I didn't want to get involved in anything this complex. I just wanted to get the point of the tip across with a simple example and I failed. At least there were 555 other tips that nobody was complaining about.

Maybe the misery was over? Not quite — there were several more letters. One lady wanted to know if I could get her Bill Root's latest book on the play of the hand! Was this a safety-play request? Another lady sent in a blank check. She asked me to send her live-in boyfriend (who had fifty masterpoints) several of my books but not 'lesson plans'. She told me that she wanted him to think he was enjoying himself, even though he is 'double-dummy hopeless'.

A third lady, who had read a review column depicting the play of the three notrump hand where I had the errant ♡10 in dummy instead of a small one, said that she was thrilled with my line of play and ordered two books.

Short, Anyway

When I asked *Bridge World* editor Jeff Rubens at a Nationals in Vancouver if he wanted an article on the tournament, he answered, "Only if it is short and funny." Well, the first part of the request was easy.

In order to appreciate the following deal. you must be aware of the prelude. I was playing with Bob Hamman in the Men's Teams, and before the event I corralled him into taking a walk to the zoo in beautiful Stanley Park. On the way, the discussion turned to bridge and for the umpteenth time, he expounded his theories of being a practical player at the bridge table; bringing up hands from years ago where I (as his partner) had failed to heed his advice. I nodded. Then he mentioned a few hands that he had bid and played recently with the practical view in mind. I nodded. Then he told me about various other experts who would be getting much better results if they were a bit more practical. I nodded. After this two-sided conversation, we sat down to do battle.

Our first opponents, upon seeing us play together for the first time in many a moon, asked us how come we were a partnership again. Hamman replied, "We both lost bets." The deal in question was not the first we played in the event. It was the second. First, I will give you my hand as a problem. You are sitting North, vulnerable against not, when your partner deals and passes and your right-hand opponent opens three diamonds. This is your hand:

♠ A Q J 9   ♡ Q   ◇ A 9 2   ♣ K Q J 9 8

What would you bid?

"What was the practical bid?" I asked myself. None came to mind, so I bid what I thought was right, three notrump. this was passed on my left; and after a lengthy pause, Hamman bid four hearts, just what I wanted to hear. This was passed around to my left-hand opponent, who doubled. The bidding came back to me:

WEST	NORTH	EAST	SOUTH
	Me		*Hamman*
			pass
3◇	3NT	pass	4♡
pass	pass	dbl	pass
pass	?		

I knew that Bob had six hearts, but why didn't he open a Weak Two? Obviously his hearts weren't that good or, perhaps he had a heart-club two-suiter with five cards in each suit, or perhaps, six hearts and four spades. In any case, I convinced myself that four hearts doubled was not the right contract. Now what was I to do—in a practical vein of course.

I reasoned that in this event with board-a-match scoring, a redouble by me would surely be for takeout — as simply passing and making four hearts doubled would insure a win on the board. I made a rescue redouble. Everyone passed.

NORTH
♠ A Q J 9
♡ Q
◇ A 9 2
♣ K Q J 9 8

SOUTH *(Hamman)*
♠ 4 3
♡ K 10 7 6 5 4
◇ Q
♣ A 10 5 3

Opening Lead: ◇ J

Before describing the intricacies of the play, I think it only fair that you know a bit more about the personality of lovable Bob. When he used to live in Los Angeles, he played a tremendous amount of rubber bridge, and he was a winner; a big winner; but that wasn't all. He used to needle his opponents after he beat them. You would think that this combination of losing money while getting insulted would make them look for another game. No. Actually, the reverse took place. Everyone wanted to play in Hamman's game. The revenge motive.

Once a theoretical question was posed at the club: "If you were playing in a pivot game with Hamman, would you rather win thirty dollars and see Hamman win fifty dollars, or lose thirty dollars while seeing Hamman lose fifty dollars?" Never was there such unanimity of opinion. To a man, everyone would rather have lost the thirty dollars.

Now for the play. Bob got off to a fast start by winning the opening diamond lead with the queen as East signaled with the eight. A low heart went to the queen and East's ace; a club came back.

The problem, as Hamman saw it, was to make the hand in case East had four or even five trumps to the A-J-9. Accordingly, he won the king of clubs in dummy and played a second club. West ruffed!

West now returned the king of diamonds to dummy's ace, as East completed the echo and Hamman discarded his losing spade. Next came the ace and queen of spades, covered by the king and ruffed by Bob as West played the ten.

At this point, Hamman reasoned that if East started with four hearts to the ace-jack, then East was a dead duck. Dummy could be entered with a club, a club discarded on the jack of spades, an the nine of spades ruffed in the closed hand, leaving Bob with K-10-7 of hearts. He could now exit with a low heart and take the last two tricks.

There were two advantages to this line of play. First, the kibitzers and I would both be impressed, and second, Hamman would not have to explain why he didn't retreat to five clubs as I had asked.

Confidently, Bob led a third club. West ruffed! East still had to make his jack of hearts, and we were down one redoubled on a hand that was cold for five. trumps had broken 3-3 all along.

Of course a practical player like Bob would never allow for West's ten of spades to be an honest card, in which case, West would have started with 2-3-7-1 distribution. In any case, I heart practical Bob mutter after the hand was over, "Three trumps and a singleton club, and he leads a diamond!"

Well, the article was short, anyway.

The First Board

H aven't you ever wondered how or why certain people keep winning most of the bridge tournaments? We know that we can
play better, and we simply can't pin all the blame on our partners
even if they deserve it. Could it possibly be that these perennial winners know something that we don't?

I have a hunch that these winners understand the philosophy of
the 'first board'. The idea behind this philosophy is somehow to
undermine the confidence of either one or preferably both opponents on the first board, and before they can regain equilibrium, to
mow them down on the second. All well and good, but how do you
go about this?

Before I discuss some new artifices, we should review two standard gimmicks. Without these, no one can ever be a regular winner.

The first and most often employed is the 'make them feel bad'
gimmick. After the hand is over and you have carefully hacked up
another hand in two spades and the opponents are sitting up in their
chairs, you mention the fact that all along they were cold for three
hearts. Whether either one of them had enough to get into the bidding is completely irrelevant — they were cold for three hearts and
you must let them know about it. Their smiles of triumph will fade,
and you can be sure they will be in the bidding on the next hand,
whatever they have.

The second standard maneuver is not to let a bad play by the
enemy get away unnoticed. However, the trick is to time the comment properly and to deliver it in the proper tone of voice. Let's say
that West has let you make a game contract by leading the wrong suit
near the end of a rather difficult hand. You say nothing. You must
wait until the players have pulled out their cards from the next
board. Then, in an aside to East that West is 'not supposed' to hear,

you very casually mention the fact that a diamond shift by West, instead of the spade he chose, would have beaten you. Obviously, this sets up a fine mood (for you) on the second board.

I realize that I am wasting time by repeating these standard ploys but I have been working on this subject for quite a while. Now I would like to present three new plays. The first is called 'Faking a Ruff' and it goes something like this:

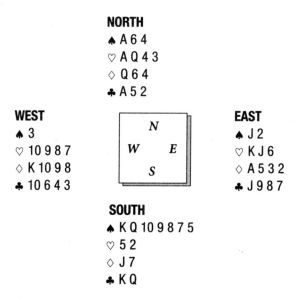

NORTH
♠ A 6 4
♡ A Q 4 3
◊ Q 6 4
♣ A 5 2

WEST
♠ 3
♡ 10 9 8 7
◊ K 10 9 8
♣ 10 6 4 3

EAST
♠ J 2
♡ K J 6
◊ A 5 3 2
♣ J 9 8 7

SOUTH
♠ K Q 10 9 8 7 5
♡ 5 2
◊ J 7
♣ K Q

You become declarer at four spades, and West leads the ten of hearts. Being a gambler at heart, you play the queen, and when this loses to the king you utter a silent prayer that East will not find the diamond shift.

East goes into a long trance and finally produces the deuce of diamonds. You play the seven and West wins with the king. West now returns the ten of diamonds. You play low from dummy and East plays the ace, which you trump. Yes, I know you are revoking, but let me finish. At this point you must make sure that you are considering your next play very seriously. Do not look up to see what is happening. I will tell you.

East is having a mini stroke. You see, he thinks his partner has returned the ten of diamonds, holding the jack! West, on the other hand, thinks that his partner must have the jack of diamonds hidden behind another card. Baleful looks are flashing across the table.

East will be the first to speak. "Have we changed our signaling system recently — like in the past five seconds, partner?" West will ignore this and slowly and deliberately ask his partner to please count his cards. East will be on the verge of an eruption (these plays should really be saved for the Mixed Pairs, come to think of it) when you innocently come to the rescue.

"Gosh!" you gasp. "Here's that jack of diamonds — it was mixed up in my hearts." The overall effect is just beautiful! First, you have made it clear to the opponents that they don't trust each other. Second, each will inwardly hate the other for alerting you to your stupid revoke. They should be easy pickings on the next board.

This ploy has interesting ramifications. Just the other day I tried it in a rubber game — and even the kibitzers stood up. Basically, the situation was this:

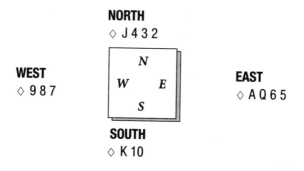

NORTH
◇ J 4 3 2

WEST
◇ 9 8 7

EAST
◇ A Q 6 5

SOUTH
◇ K 10

You are playing a spade contract, and West leads the diamond nine. You duck in dummy and East elects to play the six. You win with the ten. Then West gets the lead in another side suit and plays the eight of diamonds. This time East puts up the ace, and naturally, you trump.

Right here, East angrily announces to the kibitzers that West's proper lead from ◇ K987 was the seven, not the nine. The kibitzers snicker. They know that West is livid. He's the one who is being laughed at — when his partner was (and is) the biggest idiot of all time! Holding the ◇ AKQ, East let you win Trick 1 with the ten!

Unprintable yelling goes back and forward across the table. You let this go on for a little time before you produce the diamond king — with due apologies of course.

For those readers who are eager to know the combinations (besides those already given) that are most likely to produce blood, I suggest as a starter:

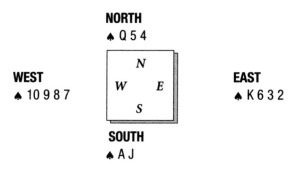

NORTH
♠ Q 5 4

WEST
♠ 10 9 8 7

EAST
♠ K 6 3 2

SOUTH
♠ A J

West leads the ten and you win with the jack. West gets in again and leads the nine. East plays low again, and you ruff. Remember, don't play anything — just ruff and wait. The rest will take care of itself, I promise you.

Next:

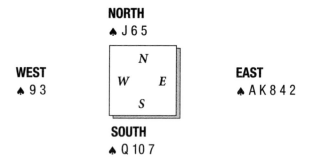

NORTH
♠ J 6 5

WEST
♠ 9 3

EAST
♠ A K 8 4 2

SOUTH
♠ Q 10 7

West leads the nine, and you drop the queen under the king. East plays the ace, and you ruff…

If these fail to produce the desired results, do not give up. 'The Advance Claim Gambit' may be lurking around the corner — a sure winner:

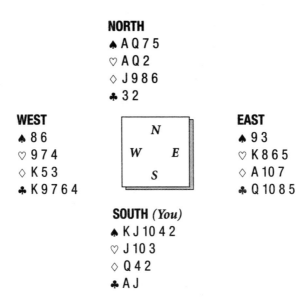

NORTH
♠ A Q 7 5
♡ A Q 2
◇ J 9 8 6
♣ 3 2

WEST
♠ 8 6
♡ 9 7 4
◇ K 5 3
♣ K 9 7 6 4

EAST
♠ 9 3
♡ K 8 6 5
◇ A 10 7
♣ Q 10 8 5

SOUTH *(You)*
♠ K J 10 4 2
♡ J 10 3
◇ Q 4 2
♣ A J

This time you are in three spades and West leads the nine of hearts. You play the queen, and East wins and shifts to a low club. You take this, draw two rounds of trumps, strip the hearts and casually lay your hand on the table announcing that you have to lose two diamonds and a club — making three. You must carefully refrain from actually leading the club and making the forced diamond return obvious.

At this point one of two things will happen:

1) Both opponents will keep their cards up, and sooner or later one will ask, "How are you going to play that diamond suit?" You look at him disdainfully and say, "I thought anybody would be able to see that baby throw-in play. I am going to lead a club and force you to play diamonds to me. Can't you see it?" you should repeat. Whoever asked now feels like the village idiot and should be mush on the next board.

2) The more likely possibility however, when you spread your hand, is that at least one opponent will expose his cards from force of habit. Both opponents will examine your hand carefully, and one is bound to blurt out, "Just how are you going to handle that diamond suit?" You look at the defender's exposed hand and say, "Well, now that

I can see who has the ten of diamonds, I will..." An uproar will ensue; the director will be summoned, but you are safe. All you have to do is to lead your club as you intended all along. It ought to take them at least one board to regain composure.

Although it is close to impossible that either of these ploys will go wrong, you still have the *coup de grâce* at your disposal, namely 'The Hidden Ball Trick':

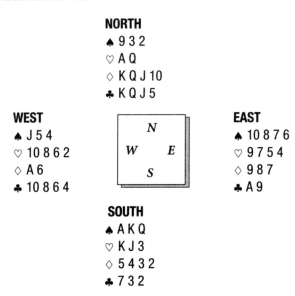

NORTH
♠ 9 3 2
♡ A Q
◇ K Q J 10
♣ K Q J 5

WEST
♠ J 5 4
♡ 10 8 6 2
◇ A 6
♣ 10 8 6 4

EAST
♠ 10 8 7 6
♡ 9 7 5 4
◇ 9 8 7
♣ A 9

SOUTH
♠ A K Q
♡ K J 3
◇ 5 4 3 2
♣ 7 3 2

This time you are playing three notrump. Your grandmother can make five in her sleep, but you battle on. West leads the deuce of hearts and you win with the queen, playing the three from your hand. East signals with the seven. You lead the king of diamonds. West wins with the ace and returns a low heart. This time you play the king under the ace, saving the jack. Now you play a couple of rounds of diamonds and West discards a heart. After all, if you don't have any more hearts West doesn't need to save both hearts, and a club or a spade discard could be costly.

The moment West discards a heart, East knows that West cannot have the jack for he would be throwing good tricks away. So actually, they are both reasoning quite well. We will definitely have to do something about that! You now lead the king of clubs from dummy.

East wins with the ace and, knowing the futility of a heart return, tries a spade. At this point you are solid. Your play is marked and you move in for the kill. You casually hide the jack of hearts behind one of your other cards and hold your hand out for everyone to see, at the same time murmuring that someone must have forgotten to cash good hearts.

East of course will be furious because West pitched a heart, holding the jack, and will demand to be told how West could have been such an idiot. West will snarl "What jack?" and upbraid East for not even knowing that he — East — had that card.

Remember, do not laugh! Let them alone. The longer they keep it up, the better your prospects become. Of course they'll finally grab your cards and locate the elusive heart jack, but the damage has been done: each is secretly aware that he doesn't really trust the other as far as he can throw the water cooler.

So — you were wondering how some people win tournaments? Shame on you. Now go out there and dazzle 'em with your footwork! But don't forget to do it on the first board!

$\mathcal{P}anel\ \mathcal{T}ime$

I had a dream. In this dream I was playing bridge when this really difficult bidding problem arose. Many knowledgeable friends agreed to its tremendous complexity. I decided to submit the problem to *The Bridge World* along with my own thoughts, and eagerly waited to see what an expert panel would come up with. *The Bridge World* confirmed my view of the problem and used it in their next issue. The panel certainly didn't disappoint me with the acuity of their analyses. Here is the problem.

Matchpoints, E-W vul. You, South, hold:

♠ 9 6 5   ♡ A K J 10 9 8   ◊ 5   ♣ K 10 5

WEST	NORTH	EAST	SOUTH
1♠	pass	2♠	?

AL ROTH: "Pass. No problem on this round. I expect the world to bid three hearts, but what do they know? It is insane to enter the bidding so soon in front of an unlimited hand. I recall a similar hand where opener had five-six in the majors and the three-heart bidders were punished severely. I do anticipate a small problem when four spades comes back to me. Table feel will see me through — it always has."

ERIC KOKISH: "Three clubs. Beverly and I play that this shows six hearts and exactly three clubs to two honors plus a singleton small diamond. Naturally, we bid three diamonds if the minor suits are reversed. This is clearly superior to a direct overcall of three hearts, which shows a singleton honor in either minor."

JEFF RUBENS: "Three diamonds. Transfer to three hearts. In my most recent *Bridge World* article, 'Kickback, Kickoff and Dropkick', I covered this sequence at great length. Three clubs is a transfer to three diamonds and two notrump shows clubs with a heart stopper. This liberates three spades to be a transfer to three notrump. The beauty of the scheme is that a direct three notrump can now be used to show four hearts plus a shorter minor.

BERKOWITZ-COHEN: "Pass. The opponents have ten trumps — eight that they know about plus two from a previous deal that they don't know about. We, on the other hand, have only six total trumps as partner is marked with a heart void given our spade length (see page 864, 8th printing — advanced distributional inferences). With sixteen total tricks available, only six of which we can take, the opponents are about to pass out a cold game.

"Incidentally, the deal contains a never-before-documented flaw, the paired minor-suit fives. This will be revealed for the first time in print in our next book, *Paired and Impaired Partners — How to Make the Proper Maladjustments*."

MAX & MARY HARDY: "Abstain. This isn't the first time you have presented us with a hand that has three fives but no five of hearts. As far as we know, only Berkowitz-Cohen are aware of the treacherous implications. Besides, the problem has nothing to do with two-over-one as a game force from here to eternity, so why bother?"

BOBBY WOLFF: "Five hearts. Experience comes into play here. This is clearly the time to exert maximum pressure. I intend to double the inevitable five spades, Lightner, demanding the lead of the ace of diamonds."

MICHAEL LAWRENCE: "Double. In my eleventh book on overcalls and doubles, I have swung around to the 'world' position of doubling with hands of this type instead of the short-sighted and impractical direct three-heart bid. Double is more flexible because it brings both minors into the picture. It goes without saying that I intend to pass a three diamond response. Unlike Zia, I do not subscribe to equal-level perversion."

JOHN LOWENTHAL: "Three notrump — unusual. I ran four simulations with Borel and each time three hearts was the clear-cut winner. On the fifth simulation, Borel told me to bid what I wanted, knowing full well I was plugging for three notrump, unusual. Borel agreed that three notrump was unusual."

MICHAEL ROSENBERG: " [...] I see this as an ethical, not a bidding problem. Did my partner hesitate even a millisecond before passing one spade? If so, I am barred. Did East have a problem before making the raise? If so, I bid three hearts as West is barred. There are other considerations: 1) how far away is the tournament director? 2) who is serving on the committee? I think committee members should be listed with the vulnerability. Otherwise, a very thoughtful problem."

ZIA: "Three hearts. A very sexy problem, probably sent in by a young woman who is hoping to hear from me. The problem, as I see it, is that the hand does not contain a queen, which enhances its sexual allure. Where are the queens and how many can I have? Oh, yes, my bid. For the time being I will content myself with a psychic three-heart overcall. Of course, I expect my all-time favorite partner, Michael Rosenberg, eventually to work out that I actually have hearts, but it won't matter. I inadvertently rubbed my chin before making the bid which, of course, barred Michael for the rest of the event."

EDGAR KAPLAN: "Pass. Although the answer to most difficult problems is to bid your longest suit, in all honesty I simply cannot get myself to do that here. Surely others have noticed the inflexibility of the trump suit (if partner has three small hearts, there is no dummy entry). This is a very bad sign. Another bad sign is the favorable vulnerability, a well known trap for overbidders. Finally, and most importantly, Norman agrees with the pass."

KIT WOOLSEY: "Two notrump, natural. This is a problem where one might expect several off-the-wall answers such as three hearts. The three-heart bidders have completely missed the subtlety of what going on here. After the expected heart lead against four spades and immediate diamond switch, declarer will be alerted to the singleton possibility. However, after my natural two-notrump overcall, declarer will play me for a balanced hand and I expect to get an early or eventual diamond ruff. It's so obvious when you think about it."

EDDIE KANTAR: "Three spades. A real toughie. EKCB (Exclusion

Key Card Blackwood) doesn't seem to apply. The difficulty, as I see it, is how to agree hearts before launching into RKCB (1430 responses). Aha! The answer is so simple that it almost eluded me. The right bid is clearly three spades, a transfer to four hearts (at this vulnerability only). Once partner bids four hearts, I shall be well placed to bid four notrump — RKCB, hearts agreed (1430 responses, or did I say that already?).

"On a more theoretical note, has anyone else noticed the forcing-pass implications running rampant throughout this problem? If I pass two spades, should that be considered forcing at this vulnerability? A more intriguing question: if West makes a game-try over two spades and partner passes, should that pass also be considered forcing? Perhaps this is a basis for a future problem..."

That's when I woke up.

The Cast Party

Each year the Westwood Unit of the ACBL in Los Angeles, my unit, has a party. The party includes an afternoon duplicate, cocktails, dinner, a show after dinner, and an evening duplicate. All this for only $300.00 per person (just kidding). Each year Phyllis Fein, the director of the show, calls and asks me (tells me) if I will be in the show. The show is always a takeoff on some Broadway musical with the lyrics by Phyllis, who must be among the top two in the world at doing this. Each year I refuse. I can't act, I can't sing, and I can't dance. Besides, I get nervous when I have to say the three or four lines that they have risked giving me. Other than that, I am perfect for the part. Each year I wind up in the show.

There was good and bad news with this year's production. The good news was that during part of the show I would be sitting at a bridge table, ostensibly practicing for the upcoming Vanderbilt with my partner, Rhoda Walsh. As a safety play, Phyllis taped my name on the seat I was to use. I noticed that no other seat had a name tag on it.

I was to play the following hand, surrounded by kibitzers:

Vul: Neither
Dealer: East

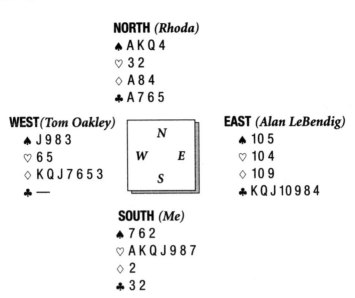

NORTH *(Rhoda)*
♠ A K Q 4
♡ 3 2
◊ A 8 4
♣ A 7 6 5

WEST *(Tom Oakley)*
♠ J 9 8 3
♡ 6 5
◊ K Q J 7 6 5 3
♣ —

EAST *(Alan LeBendig)*
♠ 10 5
♡ 10 4
◊ 10 9
♣ K Q J 10 9 8 4

SOUTH *(Me)*
♠ 7 6 2
♡ A K Q J 9 8 7
◊ 2
♣ 3 2

The kibitzers were all told to watch how carefully we bid and played each hand. Our careful bidding was: three clubs from Alan, four hearts by me, five diamonds by Tom, and a resounding seven hearts from Rhoda, which ended the auction. Tom led the ◊ K. Winning with the ace, I threw my cards on the table with a flourish, claiming thirteen tricks — even though there were only twelve top tricks. I announced that I was going to draw trumps, cross to the ♠A, ruff a diamond, isolating the diamond menace, and play off all of my trumps, eventually executing a double squeeze if either opponent happened to have four spades. Of course, I knew this line of play would work because I had made up the hand.

The good news on the play was that I didn't blow any of my lines. The bad news was that this musical ended with everyone doing a dance step that we had rehearsed at length, but one that I had never 'quite' mastered. Fortunately, there were so many people on stage for the grand finale that we had to form two lines. I immediately sprinted to the back line in order to stand behind Harvey Goodman, the tallest person in the play. Unfortunately, Harvey knows how to dance and he actually did the number, which required moving from side to side. When he did this, I was in big trouble, a fact that did not go unnoticed by certain members of the audience. Nonetheless, the show was a success. Everyone clapped. For another year I wouldn't have to worry about one of these 'galas'.

A few weeks after the show I got a call from Phyllis on my answering machine. "We are going to have cast party. It is going to be at Goldie Jacobson's home."

Goldie is the best cake maker in the world. Whenever I write a new book, I trade a copy for a cake. Neither of us can believe what a good deal we are getting. In any case, attendance is compulsory. Furthermore, everyone must bring either something to eat or contribute $10.00. I called Phyllis back and got her machine. I told her that I would bring a dessert. Why I would choose to bring a dessert to Goldie's house is beyond me, but this is what I chose to do at the time. I asked the machine if that was O.K. The next day I got this letter in the mail:

My Dear Edwin,

Of course you may bring a dessert if you wish,
Like blueberry muffins or pie in a dish,
Pineapple pudding of course would be nice,
Or the pudding that's made with raisins and rice,

How 'bout some taffy or maybe some truffles,
Or green party mints on a doily with ruffles
A big chocolate mousse or a real pecan pie,
Or strawberry tarts with whipped cream on high.

The choices are endless for desserts you can bring.
(My suggestions are free, they won't cost a thing),
But do understand they are only suggestions —
You bring what you want, without any questions.

If it's home-made, of course, or if you should buy it,
The cast at the party will certainly try it.
But Eddie (and I do hope this won't make you frown),
If it's home-made by you, we all may leave town!

With much sincerity,
Phyllis

After the party, Phyllis told me she was counting on me for next year's show. I refused. I absolutely refused. No way on earth am I going to go through that trauma again.

Stay tuned to see how well I do in the next show.

Travel

For Eddie, it's not a Game — it's a Wild Adventure!

I get these invitations. This one came in the mail sometime in June inviting me and a partner of my choice to a newly organized tournament to be held in December in Manchester, England. The format was to be two one-day pair games. I asked one of my best friends, Don Krauss, to play, and he accepted.

About four days before our scheduled departure, a headline caught my attention: 'Worst Blizzards in History Ravage Great Britain'. Underneath was a horror story about people being stuck for hours or even days in Heathrow trying to get out. I decided to call my newly-married friend, Rob Sheehan, to find out how bad it really was.

He told me not to worry — most of the roads were in order. And besides, he had invited some friends over to dinner the night of our arrival and didn't want to disappoint them. I said I would call him back in a couple of days.

On the day of the flight I called back armed with a few more 'chilling' reports of what was going on there. This time Robert told me it was sunny and to stop being such a fuss-budget.

O.K., we said, we'd go. Suddenly Krauss, a stockbroker, was faced with a very sticky decision. A very important transaction that meant much to Don was in the offing and it was absolutely necessary that he be in town or else possibly lose the deal. What to do? Perhaps, he said, I could find a substitute? On the day of the flight?

Not to worry — I know Billy Eisenberg, don't I? Billy the Kid. The only person alive who could rearrange his life in nine hours. Instead of going to the club from work he went to Europe!

We went prepared: mittens, scarves, ski jackets, thermal underwear, the works. It didn't matter. We have California blood in our veins these days. We froze to death. Sheehan and his sunny London!

The plan was to arrive in London at noon, have dinner at Sheehan's and take the train to Manchester the following afternoon.

Five of us made the trek — Sheehan and his wife, Penny; one of his regular partners, the brilliant Pakistani, Zia Mahmood (who Sheehan swears is one of the two best rubber bridge players in the world); plus Billy and me.

While Penny and Zia were engaged in some head-to-head backgammon, Billy and I were merrily misbidding hands. What else is new? Finally, we arrived... and was it cold!

Zia was to have called Paul Hackett to tell him exactly what time we were arriving. Someone was supposed to meet us at the station and take us to our respective hotels. Zia forgot to call.

Well, we could always take a cab, couldn't we? Not so fast, Charlie. In Manchester the queue (notice new vocabulary creeping in) was single file outside the train depot to catch a cab. The line was long — very long — so we decided to walk.

In fairness to Billy I must say this — his suitcase was heavier than any of the others. Billy, therefore, was always about a half block behind the rest of us.

After about a five-block hike we arrived at *their* hotel. *They* immediately went to their rooms, leaving us to fend for ourselves, a tragic mistake.

We knew we were looking for the St. James Club and we even had the address. We wanted to call up but our hands were too cold to use the telephone directory.

Finally a stranger dialed the number for us but no one answered. Not to worry. We were told it was only a few blocks away and we were pointed in the right direction. We had only to find Charlotte St. and turn right.

We walked about four blocks and still no Charlotte St. We were now reduced to asking someone else what had happened to Charlotte St. Apparently nothing had happened to it — we had passed it! We couldn't believe it. We were too cold to believe it.

We headed back the same way, and sure enough there was a sign

that said Charlotte St. You could only see the sign from one direction. The street sign was blank on the other side!

Now all we had to do was find the St. James Club. Keep in mind that it was dark outside. We missed it! To bring a miserable story to an end, it took us exactly forty-five minutes to find the St. James Club. The next morning, when we could see where we were going, we realized that the St. James Club was less than a block away from *their* hotel. People who know Billy and me (particularly Billy) will not find this story hard to believe.

Now we had to rush to make the reception. Brother, did they ever get a raft of experts for this event. I hope I don't exclude anybody but the field had: Sharif, Chemla, Stoppa, Desrousseaux, Farahat and Renouard from France. Kelsey and McMonagle from Scotland; Mervis and Calderwood from South Africa; Werdelin and Norris from Denmark; Sundelin and Lindkvist from Sweden; Silverstone, Dixon, Alder, Mahmood, Hoffman, Hackett, Collings, Sowter and Lodge from England. The last four players all represented Great Britain in the last World Championship.

I bet you are wondering if I am ever going to get around to any hands. Patience.

The first day Billy and I wound up fifth. The winners were Silverstone and Dixon of Great Britain. My one hand is from the second day's play — but first, an introductory story.

You see, there are two things I still haven't mentioned. (1) This event was being shown on Vugraph a few miles away at the University of Manchester, and (2) as an added attraction four of the invited pairs — Chemla-Sharif, Sundelin-Lindkvist, Collings-Hackett and Eisenberg-Kantar — were all competing for the NatWest Trophy. This went to the pair who had the best board-a-match result against the other three pairs spanning the entire two days.

Entering the evening session of the second day, Billy and I were on Vugraph facing Collings and Hackett. We had started against them the previous day as well and we were still looking for our first matchpoint.

In fact, Billy and I had noticed that we invariably got a zero on the first and last board of every session. The commentator asked us to say a few words into the mike. I said that I did not want to get another 'first round' zero and was going to play for an average. Billy echoed this — in spades.

With both sides vulnerable, sitting North, I gazed at the following collection wondering how I was ever going to get an average with:

♠ Q 8 7 4 2   ♡ 9 8   ◇ A K 7 6 3 2   ♣ —

I decided to pass and the bidding developed quickly:

WEST	NORTH	EAST	SOUTH
Collings	*Me*	*Hackett*	*Billy*
	pass	4♡	dbl
pass	?		

Before you decide on your bid, you are entitled to know that we play a double of 4♡ shows spades — except when it doesn't. If it doesn't, the doubler has a mountain. O.K., what do you bid?

I decided on 5♠! This was raised to 6♠ and doubled by Collings amidst laughter! Billy ran to 6NT which was also doubled by Collings. More laughter. A heart was led and this was the entire deal:

NORTH
♠ Q 8 7 4 2
♡ 9 8
♢ A K 7 6 3 2
♣ —

WEST
♠ K 10 5 3
♡ 5 3
♢ 10 9 8 5
♣ J 10 8

```
     N
  W     E
     S
```

EAST
♠ J 6
♡ K Q J 10 7 6 4
♢ —
♣ Q 6 5 4

SOUTH
♠ A 9
♡ A 2
♢ Q J 4
♣ A K 9 7 3 2

Billy ducked the heart opening, won the continuation and played ace and a spade. Collings won the king and Billy spread his hand. Down one doubled and vulnerable — another zero!

Let me add that Dixon, sitting West, defended 6♢ by North on a heart lead. At Trick 2 declarer dumped a heart on the ♣A and played ace and a spade. Dixon ducked. Declarer, fearing a doubleton king in the East hand, also ducked. After East made his jack and trumps turned out to be 4-0, declarer could not ruff two spades in dummy without losing a trump trick. Nice play. Back to the conversation.

"Billy, I thought we promised spades when we doubled 4♡."

"Well, what did you want me to do with this hand, pass?"

"No, but why did you raise me to six?"

"I thought you had ♠KQJxx. After all, you were a passed hand."

"Why do you always play me for just the hand you want me to have?" (Very important to say this before he does.)

"Well, you might have bid your ace-king-sixth suit, you know."

"Well, why didn't you bid yours?" For once I felt I had come out of one of these verbal exchanges with a winning draw.

Billy and I won the NatWest Trophy. Of course we missed our plane coming home, but that's another story.

Abandon Ship

The feeding frenzy is over. Mercifully, after two weeks the cruise ship finally docked. It's amazing how much one can put away when the food is free. As you might have guessed, I was the guest lecturer (teacher) on this luxury cruise to the Fjords. (Go if you can afford it, teach if you can't.) It's amazing the God-like aura that bridge teachers seem to have to the cruise passengers, while management considers them one step removed from steerage. After all, they take up cabin space and are constantly asking for favors (markers, cards, a microphone, more time to use the card room, etc.). The teacher (me) is also expected to give heady advice when he saunters into the card room and finds some class attendees playing rubber bridge. For example, what should I have advised someone who was dealer and had called me over as he gazed at this balanced hand:

♠ K 9 7 4 3 2   ♡ Q   ◇ K 8 6 4 3 2   ♣ —

Not having my usual advantage of knowing all four hands, I advised him to pass. His partner opened one heart and I hung around to see what would happen. RHO overcalled three clubs and 'we' bid three spades. Partner rebid three notrump which 'we' corrected to four diamonds. Partner continued with four hearts. Up to then, I had been on fairly firm ground, but things were getting a bit hairy. I think I should have had the guy bid five diamonds, but I told him to bid four spades. This was greeted by four notrump.

Four notrump in a classroom situation is always Blackwood. It is never natural and it is never Key Card. I fell from grace. I had the guy bid five diamonds over his partner's four notrump. Yes, I was swimming. I could always mutter something about Key Card, or lower myself in my own eyes beyond compare and mention the void if it came to that. Partner then leapt to six spades, which was doubled by the player on lead.

The opening lead was the ♡A and dummy tabled:

♠ A 10   ♡ K J 10 7 5   ◇ A Q J   ♣ A 8 7

Six spades was not a great success with six diamonds on ice. My guy played the hand beautifully. He won the club shift with the ace and led the ♠10 from dummy as I tried not to cringe. It didn't matter, I guess. His RHO had the stiff jack so he went down two. Curiously, that was the last time that guy asked me for advice during the entire cruise.

Since instructors are not allowed to play in the afternoon duplicate, I sometimes fill in as a fourth for rubber bridge. (Not everyone gets to the game on time and some prefer rubber bridge).

Vul: Neither
Dealer: West
Cruise Bridge (Translation: anything might happen.)

NORTH
♠ K J 10 4
♡ K 8 4 3
♢ K J 6 5
♣ Q

SOUTH *(teacher)*
♠ 9 8 5 3
♡ 2
♢ Q 7 4 3
♣ K J 9 5

North Sea auction:

WEST	NORTH	EAST	SOUTH
1♡[1]	double	2♡	2♠[2]
all pass			

1. Five-card suit
2. One word from teacher usually ends all auctions

Opening Lead: ♢A

East played the ♢9 and West immediately shifted to a low club. East won the ace and returned the ♢2, which I won in my hand, West playing the ♢10. Question: who had the ♢8? East, a beginner, would never play the ♢9 from the ♢982; but why would West with ♢A108 lead the ♢A and if she did, why would she shift after partner played the ♢9? And would West really play the ♢10 from an original holding of ♢A108? In this game, nobody 'wastes' high cards.

Strange. I knew was being threatened with a diamond ruff, but I didn't know who was threatening me! The truth of the matter was that I actually thought the ◊8 must be on the floor. I even took a look. It wasn't. One of them had it!

Not to worry, I knew how to avoid a ruff in this position. After all, I'm the teacher. I led a spade to the king. West figured to have the ace and I was willing to give up two spades and three aces. Not so fast. *East* took the ♠A! Would the elusive ◊8 be coming back? No, a heart came back to West's ace. Now, out of nowhere, came the ◊8, ruffed by East. West's original doubleton ♠Q became the setting trick. Would you like to see all four hands?

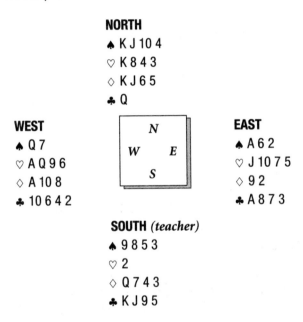

NORTH
♠ K J 10 4
♡ K 8 4 3
◊ K J 6 5
♣ Q

WEST
♠ Q 7
♡ A Q 9 6
◊ A 10 8
♣ 10 6 4 2

EAST
♠ A 6 2
♡ J 10 7 5
◊ 9 2
♣ A 8 7 3

SOUTH *(teacher)*
♠ 9 8 5 3
♡ 2
◊ Q 7 4 3
♣ K J 9 5

What happened to West's fifth heart? She had missorted her hand and the ◊8 was in with her hearts. She thought she was leading from ◊A10 doubleton. So why didn't she continue with a diamond? Because once she found the eight of diamonds, she could no longer get a ruff. It's all so obvious. And don't even ask about East's bidding.

Keep the faith.

Cruising Along

$\diamondsuit$

Once a year I give bridge lectures on a Cunard line cruise ship. The lectures take place in the mornings while the ship is at sea. An ACBL-accredited duplicate game follows in mid-afternoon. Following the duplicate I usually get questions. Most of the questions deal with bids (partner's bids, what else?) but every so often someone comes up with a play problem. These 'play problems' I can usually dispose of in seconds. Usually.

My good friend, Bob Granum of Alpena, Michigan, who has been coming to my various Mexican bridge vacation outings for a while, decided that I hadn't confused him enough in North America so he and his family were now trying me out in the Mediterranean. Anyway, Bob hit me with this little number that you see on the next page. Not only that, he showed me all four hands! I must really be slipping. Anyway, I was prepared to answer the question in seconds. O.K., minutes. O.K., a quarter of an hour. All right, I told Bob I would let him know the answer at lunch. My credibility was shrinking by the minute.

This was the hand:

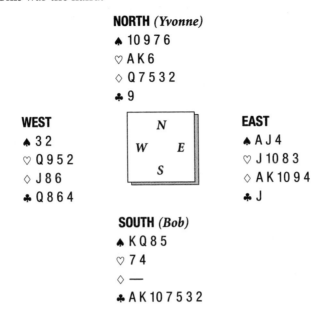

NORTH *(Yvonne)*
♠ 10 9 7 6
♡ A K 6
◇ Q 7 5 3 2
♣ 9

WEST
♠ 3 2
♡ Q 9 5 2
◇ J 8 6
♣ Q 8 6 4

EAST
♠ A J 4
♡ J 10 8 3
◇ A K 10 9 4
♣ J

SOUTH *(Bob)*
♠ K Q 8 5
♡ 7 4
◇ —
♣ A K 10 7 5 3 2

It seems that Bob, playing with the lovely Yvonne, was the only South to arrive at a spade contract: four spades to be exact. Everyone else played in clubs making four. Had Bob been able to make the hand, they would have won. Alas, he went down with a trump lead, East playing low. Bob asked me if he could have made the hand. Well? What say you before reading on?

There is no room to go over all the variations in play and defense — East overruffing or not if South starts by cashing the ♣A and ruffing a club (he shouldn't). My conclusion was that if South ducks a club at Trick 2, he will prevail. East wins the ♣J and plays a high diamond, South ruffs, and ruffs a club low. If East overruffs and plays a high diamond, South ruffs and begins to play winning clubs. If East discards, South plays a spade to the ace, discards if East plays another high diamond, and claims. East-West have no answer.

If West wins the first club and leads a diamond, South ruffs and plays winning clubs, discarding red cards from dummy. No matter how East plays on those clubs, East can make only two more tricks. You circle the cards for a while, I'm exhausted.

Humiliated by how long this hand took me to analyze, I tried to avoid Bob the next day, but he found me and gave me another hand from the afternoon duplicate. I thought to myself, this can't be happening to me two days in a row. Not on a cruise, for God's sake. Again he was showing me all four hands! A very bad sign. This time Bob had taken the push to three spades after his partner had made a Michaels two-diamond overcall of West's opening one-diamond bid. West led the ♡Q and Bob went down again. He asked me if he could have made it, and again, I could not answer immediately.

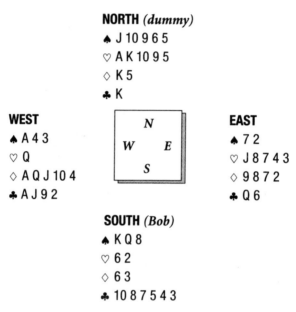

NORTH *(dummy)*
♠ J 10 9 6 5
♡ A K 10 9 5
♢ K 5
♣ K

WEST
♠ A 4 3
♡ Q
♢ A Q J 10 4
♣ A J 9 2

EAST
♠ 7 2
♡ J 8 7 4 3
♢ 9 8 7 2
♣ Q 6

SOUTH *(Bob)*
♠ K Q 8
♡ 6 2
♢ 6 3
♣ 10 8 7 5 4 3

Say you win the opening lead in dummy and lead a spade to the king, which West ducks. You continue with a low heart to the king. West discarding a middle diamond (best), and ruff a low heart with the ♠Q, West discarding a low club. At this point you must lead a diamond towards the king or you will have to lead one from dummy later! West plays a middle honor and you win the king. If you exit dummy with a trump, West wins, leads a low diamond to East's ♢9, watches East cash the ♡J, and ruffs East's heart return. Down one.

So after winning the ♢K, you must exit a diamond while still holding a trump in your hand. Triumph! Or have I blown this one?

Bob, it was nice knowing you.

The Paris-Israel Connection

As long as they keep inviting us, we'll keep going. This time Billy Eisenberg and I were invited to take part in two money tournaments. The first was in Paris — the famous Del Duca tournament, beautifully organized by the late Dr. Pierre Jais, held June 6-7. The second was in Israel, in Caesarea to be exact, from June 8-13.

We arrived in Paris a few days early to beat the jet lag. It didn't help. After a strong first session, we only had about an average game in the second session, so even though they paid down to fifty places, our names were nowhere to be seen on the prize list.

We did have our moments, however, some good and some bad. Might as well get the horror story out of the way. Of course, you have to understand when you play in a European tournament, you expect to get at least one awful result because either you or your partner will mistake one honor card for another due to a lack of familiarity with the French playing cards.

This time it was Billy. Of course, I should have been prepared because the last time we played in Europe he got mad at me for not covering dummy's queen with my jack. This time he was West and I was East and these were our cards:

WEST (*Billy*)		**EAST**(*Me*)
(blind as a bat)	N	(helpless victim)
♠ Q J 10 8 7	W E	♠ A
♡ A J 10 8 3 2	S	♡ Q 5
◊ J 4		◊ Q 10
♣ —		♣ A K Q J 8 7 4 3

With both sides vulnerable, Billy thought he had the spade king-queen and decided to open the hand with one spade. I tried a jump to three clubs which showed one of three types of hand: (1) a long solid-like club suit; (2) a notrump-type hand with a five- or six-card club suit; (3) a spade fit.

In any case, we play that a new suit by the opener now shows two of the top three honors with no reference to length. So what could poor Billy do? He decided to rebid three spades. I bid four clubs, and he persisted with four spades. Do you like this system?

Breaking all the Blackwood rules, I tried four notrump. When Billy responded, I launched straight away into six notrump. The lady on lead tried the diamond ace from Axx. Six diamond tricks later, I was down five, vulnerable.

Even though we didn't scratch in Paris, we could hardly call it a bad trip. Not only was the weather perfect, but Billy and I were wined and dined. A word to the wise: Ami Louis, 123 Rue de Bois Vert. If I were you, I wouldn't turn down an invitation to L'Orangerie either.

Billy and I were invited to L'Orangerie by the Brazilian bridge whiz, Gabriel Chagas. Gabriel now represents a Brazilian soybean company that does much of its business in France. As Gabriel is very personable and speaks eleven languages fluently, he frequently finds himself in Paris. He even has a chauffeur at his disposal. His chauffeur is so elegant that Gabriel sometimes finds himself calling the chauffeur, 'Sir'.

At dinner, he told us of his pre-soybean gambling days. Once he was involved in a high-stakes poker game when his wife called. This was strictly forbidden. She was not supposed to call him during this game. As it turned out, he was losing heavily, and the call for him to bring home some milk for the baby did not go over very well with him. In fact, he lost a fortune that night.

When he came home (seething) to his wife, he told her that he had some good news and some bad news for her. "The good news is that I brought home the milk; the bad news is that I have just lost our apartment." It was true! But his friends bailed him out. Now, of course, he has no financial worries.

The second leg of our trip was a brand new tournament organized by Armand Cohen, a non-bridge player who was interested in promoting events of this kind in Israel. He is a dentist who lives in Paris but travels frequently to Israel and even has a home in Caesarea, a small town on the Mediterranean in the northern part of Israel. Armand has more enthusiasm in his little finger than most of us can conjure up in a lifetime. What a week he showed us in Caesarea! But I am getting a bit ahead of myself.

The day that we were to leave Paris I glanced at my precious *International Herald Tribune*, my lifeline to my other world, the world where my beloved Lakers were playing for the NBA championship (without me), and Holmes and Cooney were fighting for the heavyweight title without waiting for me to get back. Silent agony.

The headlines were a bit disturbing that day. 'Israel attacks Lebanon — full-scale war in progress.' This is where I was going? As a safety play, I called the State Department. Maybe there had been a misprint in the paper. No, no misprint. In fact, they even said, don't go — it is dangerous there.

"Billy," I said, "there is a war going on — why should we go? We don't need the master points." I knew I was talking to the wrong person.

"Not to worry," Billy said, "everything will be O.K."

Armand was already in Israel, so I called his wife. She said Armand had just called and told her it was safe. I called the two

French players who were also invited, Paul Chemla and Christian Mari. Their response was very reassuring: "If we die, we die."

So of course we went. The cab driver, a friend of Armand, told us that Caesarea was about ninety minutes by cab from the fighting. We thanked him for that little tidbit of information, at the same time telling him that we weren't interested in getting any closer.

Well, there we were at the Dan Caesarea, a truly beautiful hotel, once used as a Club Med facility and guess what — not too many people showed up. Everybody was fighting in the war. In Israel, everybody fights.

Have you ever seen the bumper sticker that says, 'What if they gave a war and nobody came?' In Israel they should have one that reads, 'What if they gave a bridge tournament and everyone went to war?'

As we arrived one day after the three-session pair game had begun, the director, Israel Erdenbaum, said he would average our two remaining scores and use that as a barometer for our missing session.

The good news is that we won the tournament by a mile; the bad news is that they cancelled the prize money because so few people had shown up. Oh well, they are going to hold this tournament again next year, and without a war it should be something else.

There were a few language problems. Armand, Paul, and Christian all speak English rather well but prefer, of course, to speak French. Billy's French is such that they were forced to speak English, however, and some strange sentence constructs were heard. Once Billy double faulted, playing tennis against Christian.

Christian said, "I am very sorry."

Billy answered, in French, "I am worse sorry."

On another occasion, "Do you have money on you?"

"Yes, I have many money."

And, "Please open more the window."

By the way, this is the way we were speaking English, not the French!

What a trip!

Safari Bridge

Some years ago my then girlfriend Judy, who worked for American Airlines, asked me if I would like to go on a safari. I thought she was kidding. Until then I was happy watching Lorne Greene on the tube telling me about those wild animals. Of course we went. But we decided to do it right and visit some friends as well.

The trip started in London, where we stayed at the flat (notice how I pick up the lingo) of my good friend and British internationalist, Robert Sheehan. In fact, Robert is such a good friend that he moved out of his own place and into a friend's flat during our stay. I wouldn't say he was happy to see us leave, but on the last morning of our stay he phoned and asked me to remove some chicken from the freezer — one piece.

The highlight of the stay in London was dinner with my good friend Jonathan Cansino, who seemed to be doing quite well after some serious brain surgery. Jonathan, by the way, before the surgery was one of the best bridge players in the world. I know, I played with him quite a bit.

I might as well throw in two of my favorite Cansino stories here. The first takes place in Denver where we were playing in the Open Pairs in an extremely noisy room. Jonathan opened with four spades, holding eight spades to the K-Q-J-10; the opponents wound up in five hearts, doubled by me, only Jonathan thought that the final contract was five notrump doubled.

He led the king of spades and dummy won the singleton ace of spades (declarer and I each had a small doubleton). I got the lead at Trick 2 and began pondering what I should do next. I finally decided to force the dummy with a spade. I played my spade. At this point, Jonathan, who was still defending five notrump doubled, said, "What took you so bloody long?"

Although declarer ruffed in dummy, Jonathan proceeded to 'run' his spades, revoking five times before we sorted out what had happened. Oh well, we couldn't beat five hearts doubled anyway.

Over the years Jonathan has played quite successfully with Robert Sheehan, one of Great Britain's finest players. It so happened that after one particularly disastrous session they weren't speaking to each other at all. Finally, Sheehan approached Jonathan with a small piece of blank paper and said, "Here, Jonathan, write down all you know about bridge."

Jonathan replied, "Well, it's a bigger piece of paper than I would have given you."

The next leg of the trip was Nairobi, Kenya, for a seven-day safari. By the way, safaris these days are limited to hunting with cameras. You don't shoot them, they don't eat you. It all works out nicely.

From Nairobi we went to *bella* Roma via Athens because Alitalia was on one of its twenty-four-hour strikes that lasted thirteen days. Once at the hotel, I decided to call Giorgio Belladonna because 1) I knew he owned a bridge club and 2) he had beaten me twice in the World Championships. We had to be good friends.

Wonder of wonders, he was home and invited Judy and me to dinner at his club the following night when they had their big team game.

Now for a word about the players in the team game. Benito Garozzo and Lea du Pont had just left Turin and were moving into Giorgio's club. They, along with Georgio and me, were to play against an Italian team that was preparing for a play-off to determine Italy's representatives in the European Championships a few months later.

I was to play the first half with Giorgio. Benito and Lea would play their special Precision system that only two people in the world are capable of remembering — and they haven't found those people yet.

The way that Giorgio tells it, when he plays this system with Benito and puts his dummy down, Benito asks Lea, who is always kibitzing, to check in the 'book' to see whether or not Giorgio has bid properly! Giorgio and I decided to play *naturale* with Giorgio looking to the heavens after making this concession. Things were going along fairly well when I picked up vulnerable against not:

♠ Q ♡ A K ◇ A K J 10 6 5 ♣ 7 5 3 2

I was sitting South against a pair using the Roman Club, and the bidding went:

WEST	NORTH	EAST	SOUTH
			Me
1NT	pass	2♡	3◇
pass	pass	3♠	?

As usual, I didn't know what to do, so I tried three notrump. It went pass on my left and Giorgio bid four clubs. Now I didn't know whether he thought I had clubs or whether he had clubs. Wonderful. I decided to raise to five clubs. This was greeted by a rather vicious *contro* (we were bidding in English until then) on my left and everyone passed.

The lead was made and I asked Giorgio if I could see his hand. This is what I saw:

♠ A 6 4 2 ♡ 9 7 3 ◇ 3 2 ♣ 9 8 6 4

We were off 150 honors in clubs for openers. No matter how the clubs were divided, I knew I would not be invited back for another dinner (I was).

Furthermore, if clubs were four-one, I might not have enough lira to get out of the club, never mind out of the country. Fortunately, clubs were three-two and Giorgio managed to get out for down one, allowing his partner to breathe once again.

Nevertheless, our team was down 20 IMPs at the half, so we decided to switch partnerships. This time I played with Lea, with no kibitzers, and Giorgio played with Benito, with eighty kibitzers. I say this because there were so few witnesses to my finest hour. After a sequence that I would rather not admit, I arrived at a contract of three diamonds doubled with the following cards:

NORTH *(Lea)*
♠ A 8 6 5 4
♡ 2
◇ A 2
♣ A K J 9 7

WEST
♠ K J 9 2
♡ A 3
◇ K J 9 6 5
♣ Q 5

```
      N
  W       E
      S
```

EAST
♠ Q 10 3
♡ K Q 10 9 8 5
◇ 7
♣ 10 6 4

SOUTH *(Me)*
♠ 7
♡ J 7 6 4
◇ Q 10 8 4 3
♣ 8 3 2

The ace of hearts was led and I ruffed the heart continuation. I played the ace and ruffed a spade, crossed to a club and ruffed another spade. Back to a club followed by another spade ruff, East discarding a club.

At this point West is down to a trump flush and I have seven tricks. I ruffed a heart with the ace of diamonds, West underruffing, and led a club. East ruffed, but I discarded. West underruffed but had to ruff East's heart play and concede a ninth trick to my queen of diamonds. After a lovely set we discovered we had picked up 19 IMPs. As losers do, we rechecked the score a few dozen times, but finally I had to admit that I had lost a team match with Garozzo and Belladonna as teammates!

There were still a few extra days before the Nationals, so we went to New York looking for more friends to stay with. (It was sure nice to have had so many friends before this trip, because now we don't have any.) I tried calling another of my friends. You may have heard of her — Teri Garr. In fact, we call her 'Teri Garr, superstar'. She has appeared in *Tootsie* and many other hit movies. I knew her before she became famous because she lived in an apartment adjoining mine for about five years. As a matter of fact, I even took her out after she first moved in. When I took her home and wanted to kiss her goodnight, she said, "Take it easy, buddy, I'm on a year's lease." Rumor has it that she moved out to get away from me. But it didn't work — I tracked her down, and we wound up staying in her apartment in Greenwich Village.

Soon it was time to travel to the Nationals in Norfolk, Virginia. I was to play with John Mohan. The last time I played with John we played four-card majors, and our results left a little to be desired. This time I was greeted with "Five-card majors in first and second. Drury, forcing notrump, two-over-one game force, Astro, Flannery, Weak Twos, 15-17 notrump, Forcing Stayman and Jacoby. The rest of the card is yours." Thanks John. We did better but not quite good enough. We lost in the quarterfinals to the Stayman team.

At last, I was able to return to my beloved Venice Beach in Los Angeles. It had been a great trip, but, after all, there's no place like home.

The Flight Home

I couldn't remember ever being quite so tired. The night before, our team had just blown a two-board lead going into the final session of the Reisinger Board-a-Match Teams and finished sixth out of ten.

Now here it was early in the morning, the end of a long Thanksgiving weekend, and American Airlines was offering first $300.00 then $500.00 and finally $1,000.00 in vouchers to anyone who would give up his seat and take the next flight out four hours later. Only one of our group took the deal. We all wanted to go home.

I was sitting in the aisle with a vacant window seat to my left, wondering how I was going to kill four hours plus, when Pam Wittes approached. She told me she had exchanged her seat with a couple to accommodate them, and could she sit by the window. Of course.

Pam Wittes, in case you didn't know, won the World Mixed Pairs Championship in partnership with her husband Jon in Miami Beach several years ago. Coincidentally, she and Jon had just been interviewed in *Bridge Today* and I had read the interview with interest.

The gist of the article was how they dealt with each other's bridge blunders at the table. Judging from what I had read, Pam had a much better 'table temperament' than Jon, but Jon was working on improving that aspect of his game. In fact, the article said that Pam never said word one to Jon during the game. If something went wrong, she talked to him about it at home later, constructively. What a woman!

Well, there we were with four hours to kill and I couldn't sleep. I decided to do a crossword puzzle. It was such an easy one that I didn't have to ask Pam for assistance even though I thought she was aching to have a go at it.

Finally, I decided to ask her if she wanted to do a bid-'em-up from an Italian magazine. "Sure," she said I handed her a list of eight hands and explained to her that an 'R' meant a king, a 'D' a queen, and an 'F' a jack. She immediately made all the corrections in pen, and we were ready to bid. On the first hand we arrived at the top spot. We're on a roll. I thought. This was my second hand:

♠ K 8 5 3   ♡ A 3   ◇ A 8 4   ♣ 6 5 3 2

PAM	ME
1◇	1♠
2◇	?

It seemed to me that my choices were three diamonds, two notrump or three notrump. Wanting to show Pam I was no sissy, I jumped to three notrump on the strength of my fitting ace of diamonds. Pam passed.

PAM		ME
♠ A 2		♠ K 8 5 3
♡ K Q 4 2		♡ A 3
◇ Q J 10 7 3 2		◇ A 8 4
♣ 4		♣ 6 5 3 2

Had I rebid either two notrump or three diamonds we would have ended up on proper contract of five diamonds. Pam looked at my hand and noticed my clubs. "Dummy" she said, "we can make five diamonds." I apologized and we moved on. I survived hands three and four, but then there was hand five. I picked up:

♠ J 10 9   ♡ A 6   ◇ K J   ♣ A K 9 7 5 2

I opened one notrump. Pam responded two diamonds, transfer, and I rebid two hearts. Pam continued with three diamonds showing a forcing-to-game hand with hearts and diamonds. Fearing three notrump because of the spades, and not wanting to bid four clubs, which I thought would sound like a cuebid, I meekly bid three hearts. Pam bid four hearts and that ended the auction of hand five.

PAM		ME
♠ 6		♠ J 10 9
♡ K Q J 9 8		♡ A 6
◇ A Q 10 9 8		◇ K J
♣ Q 3		♣ A K 9 7 5 2

We looked at each other's hands. She noticed at once that we had a slam in three suits. "Dummy, why did you open one notrump with a six-card suit?" (In fairness, 'dummy' was said each time with affection.)

My God, I thought, this is worse than the Reisinger. What have I gotten myself into? Well, there were only three more hands. Maybe I'll survive. Sure. Hand six looked simple enough. I picked up:

♠ K 10 5 2   ♡ K 7   ◇ A J 5 2   ♣ 10 9 3

Pam opened one club and I responded one spade. She raised to two spades, which did not promise four-card support. I tried two notrump and Pam passed. Here are the two hands:

Obviously we belonged in a spade partscore.

PAM		ME
♠ A 9 4 3		♠ K 10 5 2
♡ Q 8		♡ K 7
◇ Q 6 3		◇ A J 5 2
♣ K Q 6 2		♣ 10 9 3

"You have a doubleton heart."

"So do you," I countered. "I had honors in every suit (she pointed to them) and I thought it might play easier in notrump."

"Well, you could have been right, but not this time." I said as sweetly as possible. But it wasn't easy.

Only two more hands to go and I had my confidence back. I knew that Pam was upset that she hadn't taken me back to three spades and maybe, just maybe, we could bid these next two hands to the proper contract. Sure.

At this point Danny Rotman walked by and asked, "How many hands have you bid?"

"Too many," said Pam. Her husband Jon was looking better and better to me all the time. By now, the other bridge players on the plane had heard some of the 'dummy' comments coming from our section and were beginning to mosey over. A mutual friend of ours, Kay Schulle leaned over her seat from two rows back to look at Pam's next hand — as if Pam were the one that needed moral support. Hand seven. I picked up:

♠ Q   ♡ 8 5 3   ◇ K J 10 9 5   ♣ A 7 6 3

I passed and Pam opened one heart. We played 'Drury'. Playing Drury, if you are a passed hand and have support for partner's major plus a hand too strong to raise to two of partner's major, you respond two clubs, indicating a near opening hand, typically with three-card support. I didn't think I was quite strong enough to Drury so I contented myself with a loud raise to two hearts. Pam bid four hearts, which ended our thrilling auction.

Cold for seven. I braced myself.

PAM		ME
♠ A 8 5		♠ Q
♡ A K Q 7 4 2		♡ 8 5 3
◇ A Q		◇ K J 10 9 5
♣ 8 2		♣ A 7 6 3

(with N W E S diagram between the two hands)

"Dummy, you have a Drury. We missed an easy grand slam."

This girl must have a twin sister who plays with Jon. I didn't say anything but the thought crossed my mind that perhaps, just perhaps, she might have found some rebid other than four hearts with that junior two-bid. Reading my mind, I heard her say, "I had a balanced hand and couldn't visualize a slam when all you could bid was two hearts."

Before fateful hand eight, I decided to canvas some of the better players aboard to see whether or not they would Drury with my hand. Most said they would, including Kay Schulle, now entrenched in Pam's camp of supporters. However, Billy Eisenberg, bless him, said it was a 'marginal Drury'.

Well, we were finally ready for the very last hand. I wanted to end this bid-'em-up on a happy note as I still had three hours left to spend with my understanding seat-mate.

Hand number eight. Neither side vulnerable and one spade is opened to my left. My hand:

♠ 5 3　♡ Q 10 5　◇ Q 5 3 2　♣ J 7 6 2

Pam overcalled two spades, describing a hand with five hearts and five or six cards in an unspecified minor. I decided to make the non-forcing response of three hearts. This was greeted by three spades from Pam, a cuebid indicating slam interest. I was definitely not interested in slam, so I signed off with four hearts. She now bid five clubs. The bidding had gone so far:

WEST	NORTH	EAST	SOUTH
Me		*Evil twin*	
	1♠	2♠	pass
3♡	pass	3♠	pass
4♡	pass	5♣	pass
?			

What does the evil twin want from me now? This must be her second suit and she must have a whale of a hand. I didn't have many bids left in me, and I didn't want to hear any more affectionate 'dummy' remarks so I screwed up my courage and bid six clubs.

I figured it would play better in clubs than hearts because she would be able to discard a spade from my hand on one of her hearts after drawing trumps — assuming, of course, that she had the ace of spades. I figured the bidding was over and was about to glance at her hand when I heard six diamonds from my left-hand seat belt. (I had stopped looking at her after hand five.)

If I didn't know better I would have thought that Marshall Miles had snuck into her seat and made that bid. But Marshall didn't even go to the tournament. There was no doubt about it; I was sweating. What in the @#$$%^%@ was she doing, and how could she possibly have stayed married to Jon for seventeen years, happily to boot?

Could diamonds be her second suit? If so, why didn't she bid diamonds first? I was sure we belonged in her minor, but at the seven-level? I could no longer take any chances; I took my piece of paper and canvassed all the experts in First Class, Business, Economy and Super Saver.

Most had agreed with my actions so far and were pondering about what to do next. In the meantime, Pam was shaking her head mournfully. "How could they all be such dummies? Here I am bidding my hand so beautifully, and they don't know what I'm doing."

The longer it took everyone to bid, the better I felt. Well, here goes nothing. I bid seven clubs! If her suit was diamonds, let her correct.

"Pass," she said. "Of course I have clubs, dummy." There it was. She had nailed me with the 'd' word again (without even seeing my hand).

"Could I just see your hand, Pam, dear?"

She looked up. 'Pam, dear' had alerted her to possible trouble.

PAM'S SISTER		ME
♠ A 7 6	N	♠ 5 3
♡ A K J 9 8	W E	♡ Q 10 5
◇ —	S	◇ Q 5 3 2
♣ A K Q 9 8		♣ J 7 6 2

"Well," I said, "we can make it if clubs are 2-2."

Kay Schulle piped up from Economy, "Clubs were 3-1."

"We still make it if the hand with three clubs has four hearts."

"The hand with three clubs did not have four hearts."

I fell back in my seat. Silence pervaded. Finally, Pam's sister said sweetly with a smile on her very pretty face, "Have any more bid-'em-ups, Edwin?"

I should have taken the voucher.

The Ladies

Ceci and Me

---◆---

I met Ceci three months ago* and life has just not been the same, nor will it probably ever be. Aside from everything else, Ceci adores playing bridge almost as much as she adores her cuddly Maltese, Minny, who kibitzes our games regularly with a lapside view. Throw in the sun (Ceci is an avid sun-worshipper) and you will begin to get an idea of where I fit into the picture. At the moment, I am a distant fourth and losing ground rapidly.

The only way I can possibly make it to third is to pick up some master points for Ceci. You see, winning isn't everything to Ceci, it is the only thing. Ask her how many points she has and she will answer, "Oh, who keeps track? About 80.53."

Now for a word or two about Ceci's game before I met her. She never had any formal instruction and played by the seat of her pants with pretty good results. Ceci is a lucky player. No matter what she does she somehow manages to land on her feet while her opponents and her partner look on in amazement. Now that I have entered the picture and have tried to discipline her game a bit, one can understand the trying times we are going through.

The hardest thing for me to do is to try to explain to Ceci, after one of her incredible bids has just given us another top, that perhaps it wasn't the best of all possible actions. For example, her conception of the penalty double has either advanced or set my game back some twenty-odd years. To give you an idea, Ceci believes the best penalty doubles are made when you have a fit in your partner's suit

---

* Readers will, I am sure, appreciate that this chapter was written some twenty years ago. E.K.

and not too many of the opponent's trumps. This idea seemed rather wild to me at first, but as time went by, I began to see the infinite wisdom it contained.

Vul: Both
Dealer: West

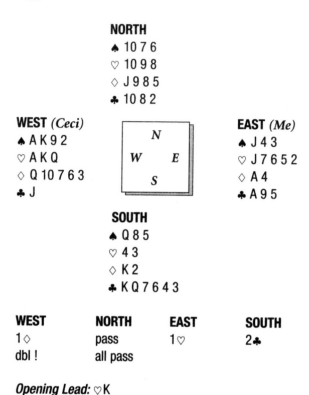

NORTH
♠ 10 7 6
♡ 10 9 8
♢ J 9 8 5
♣ 10 8 2

WEST (Ceci)
♠ A K 9 2
♡ A K Q
♢ Q 10 7 6 3
♣ J

EAST (Me)
♠ J 4 3
♡ J 7 6 5 2
♢ A 4
♣ A 9 5

SOUTH
♠ Q 8 5
♡ 4 3
♢ K 2
♣ K Q 7 6 4 3

WEST	NORTH	EAST	SOUTH
1♢	pass	1♡	2♣
dbl !	all pass		

Opening Lead: ♡K

Strangely enough, when most experts were given Ceci's hand as a rebid problem, not one found the 'obvious' double. After three rounds of hearts declarer could come up with no more than five trump tricks and went down 800 peacefully.

Tactfully I mentioned to Ceci that perhaps her trump holding left a little to be desired for such a low-level penalty double. She nodded. Only a few days later did I understand the full significance of that nod.

Vul: Both
Dealer: East

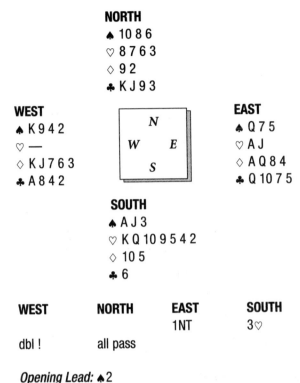

NORTH
♠ 10 8 6
♡ 8 7 6 3
♢ 9 2
♣ K J 9 3

WEST
♠ K 9 4 2
♡ —
♢ K J 7 6 3
♣ A 8 4 2

EAST
♠ Q 7 5
♡ A J
♢ A Q 8 4
♣ Q 10 7 5

SOUTH
♠ A J 3
♡ K Q 10 9 5 4 2
♢ 10 5
♣ 6

WEST	NORTH	EAST	SOUTH
		1NT	3♡
dbl !	all pass		

Opening Lead: ♠2

Guess who doubled? Of course, the hand was defeated one trick and we had no game, so all explanation was futile. However, now that I think of it, Ceci and I have a private understanding that we do not put on our convention cards. When Ceci doubles for penalties, she denies trump length. When she does have their suit, she bids notrump. Ah well, no wonder I wasn't winning anything until I met her.

To further compound this madness, Ceci tried it my way twice and doubled for penalties when she had four and five trumps. They made it both times, and as inevitable as death and taxes came, "You see what happens when you have too many trumps, they get in your way."

To try to stop Ceci from underleading aces against suit contracts is equally fruitless.

Vul: Both
Dealer: North

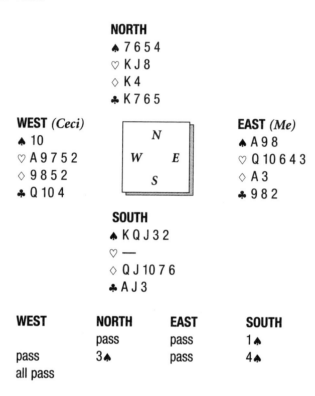

NORTH
♠ 7 6 5 4
♡ K J 8
◇ K 4
♣ K 7 6 5

WEST *(Ceci)*
♠ 10
♡ A 9 7 5 2
◇ 9 8 5 2
♣ Q 10 4

EAST *(Me)*
♠ A 9 8
♡ Q 10 6 4 3
◇ A 3
♣ 9 8 2

SOUTH
♠ K Q J 3 2
♡ —
◇ Q J 10 7 6
♣ A J 3

WEST	NORTH	EAST	SOUTH
	pass	pass	1♠
pass	3♠	pass	4♠
all pass			

Opening Lead: ♡5

After all, what else would one lead on this bidding? Declarer woodenly played the jack and ruffed my queen. The king of spades was taken by the ace and a heart returned. If declarer ruffs, he must later lose either a heart or a trump trick (by being forced to ruff a third heart with an honor) so he discarded. We were the only pair in the room to hold declarer to four.

Not having had enough success by underleading five to the ace, Ceci was now playing against the same declarer a few days later.

Vul: East-West
Dealer: East

NORTH
♠ 10 8 4 2
♡ A J 10 5
♢ A J 5
♣ K Q

WEST *(Ceci)*
♠ K
♡ 9 8 6
♢ 10 9 7
♣ A 10 8 6 4 3

```
        N
   W        E
        S
```

EAST *(Me)*
♠ A J 9 5
♡ K Q 3
♢ 6 2
♣ J 9 7 5

SOUTH
♠ Q 7 6 3
♡ 7 4 2
♢ K Q 8 4 3
♣ 2

WEST	NORTH	EAST	SOUTH
		pass	pass
pass	1♢	dbl	1♠
pass	2♠	all pass	

When I asked Ceci later why she didn't mention her clubs, she said that if she bid them and everyone passed, she would have to play the hand. For a moment I had completely forgotten how Ceci's mind works. Anyway if you don't bid a six-card suit headed by the ace-ten, you surely lead it — I mean, you surely *underlead* it! The opening lead was the six of clubs! Notice the honesty, always fourth best. Too bad the K-J doubleton wasn't in dummy, but declarer won the first trick and led a trump. I played low and declarer, placing me with the ace-king of spades, played the queen. Ceci won the king and hopefully laid down the ace of clubs which declarer ruffed. I said nothing nor did I look at Ceci (you will learn why later).

Slightly bewildered by this turn of events, declarer led another trump. I then drew all of the remaining trumps and we ran our club suit to defeat the hand three tricks. After the hand, declarer, who was still fuming, asked Ceci if she always underled aces. "Only when I have them," was the reply. One of the main reasons my position in Ceci's affections is a losing fourth is that my behavior at the bridge table is not always optimum. For example, if I violate any of the following rules (commandments), there is no telling how far downward I might spiral.

RULES FOR EDDIE TO REMEMBER
WHEN PLAYING WITH CECI

1. Always, but always, look at any dummy Ceci puts down with love and affection — no matter how hideous it might really be.
2. Never, never say a cross word or give anything but adoring looks across the table no matter how much the urge to 'kill' surges from within.
3. Never concede the rest of the tricks to the opponents even though declarer has seven cards remaining — six high trumps and an ace — and Ceci has a small trump. Somehow declarer might forget about Ceci's deuce and she might be able to trump that ace.
4. No matter how many suits Ceci bids, it does not necessarily mean she has those suits, she just wants me to bid notrump — "For God's sake, I thought you never were going to bid it."
5. Get the best possible teammates for any local event even if it means making a long-distance call to Rome for Garozzo and Belladonna.
6. Win!

We have yet to cover Ceci's play of the hand or her slam bidding. Here is an example of what goes on in my mind when I watch Ceci play a hand. I was North, and we were vulnerable.

♠ — ♡ A K 9 3 ◇ J 7 6 3 2 ♣ Q J 10 7

WEST	NORTH	EAST	SOUTH
	pass	1♠	pass
2♠	dbl	pass	2NT
pass	3◇	3♠	3NT
all pass			

Another logical auction with Ceci. I couldn't stand two notrump so, naturally, Ceci bid three notrump. And of course she doesn't double three spades so I know she must be loaded in that suit. Anyway, a spade is led and I figure that Ceci must have a big diamond fit with me (if I were playing with Marshall Miles, I would bet that he had at least five diamonds) and is counting on running that suit.

Ceci's first discard from the dummy is a diamond. Wrong again! The next card out of her hand is the queen of diamonds! First she discards one, then she plays one... Dear God, I must be going crazy! I must stop worrying about what she is doing because it almost works out. The whole deal:

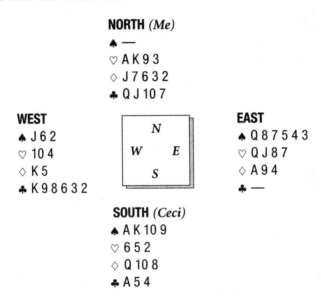

NORTH *(Me)*
♠ —
♡ A K 9 3
◇ J 7 6 3 2
♣ Q J 10 7

WEST
♠ J 6 2
♡ 10 4
◇ K 5
♣ K 9 8 6 3 2

EAST
♠ Q 8 7 5 4 3
♡ Q J 8 7
◇ A 9 4
♣ —

SOUTH *(Ceci)*
♠ A K 10 9
♡ 6 5 2
◇ Q 10 8
♣ A 5 4

When the smoke cleared, Ceci had made four notrump and was beaming. The jack of spades was led — we were playing in a tough field — and doubling three spades would hardly have been worth-while as declarer can get out for down one. Without giving you a full description of another hand Ceci played, I must tell you about her management of a suit combination.

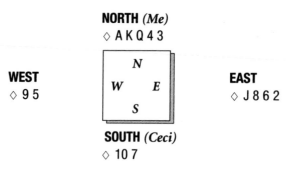

NORTH *(Me)*
◇ A K Q 4 3

WEST
◇ 9 5

EAST
◇ J 8 6 2

SOUTH *(Ceci)*
◇ 10 7

Ceci was playing a heart partial and diamonds was dummy's first-bid suit. West led the nine of diamonds. My attention wandered for a moment, and later as I looked down at the trick, I saw that Ceci had called a low diamond from dummy and had won the trick with the ten! Now I was angry at myself for not steering the hand to my beloved notrump as Ceci apparently had the jack and ten of diamonds even though I had mentioned (sweetly) that she should win these tricks with the higher of equal cards.

As Ceci pondered the dummy (a rarity) I glanced into my left-hand opponent's hand (soon to be another no-no) and lo and behold there was the jack of diamonds! Mixed emotions set in. At least Ceci had not forgotten about taking tricks with the higher of equals but how in blazes did she make her ten of diamonds, why did she duck, and how come East (a competent player) still had the jack of diamonds?

It developed that Ceci meant to call for a high diamond but she said small instead. East was so sure she was going to call for a high diamond that he also ducked and at least that mystery was solved. I hate to add this, but later in the hand, Ceci played off two high diamonds and West ruffed. West in turn put her partner back in to play the jack of diamonds, and although I'm not sure, I think Ceci finally wound up losing an extra trick by ducking the *!%&!% diamond lead in the first place.

Ceci is not beneath taking an occasional practice finesse if the situation demands it. The definition of a 'practice' finesse is, in case you are interested, a finesse which, if it works, gives you the same number of tricks you would have taken if you had not finessed at all. But it does keep you in practice.

Witness this hand:

Vul: East-West
Dealer: North

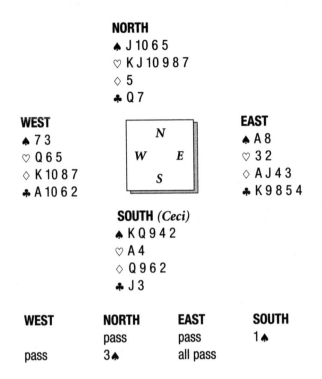

NORTH
♠ J 10 6 5
♡ K J 10 9 8 7
◇ 5
♣ Q 7

WEST
♠ 7 3
♡ Q 6 5
◇ K 10 8 7
♣ A 10 6 2

EAST
♠ A 8
♡ 3 2
◇ A J 4 3
♣ K 9 8 5 4

SOUTH (*Ceci*)
♠ K Q 9 4 2
♡ A 4
◇ Q 9 6 2
♣ J 3

WEST	NORTH	EAST	SOUTH
	pass	pass	1♠
pass	3♠	all pass	

Opening Lead: ♠3

East won the trick and returned a club to West's ace. West, a clever soul, played another trump, thus giving Ceci a chance to do a little 'practicing'. Notice that if Ceci plays the ace-king and a third heart, ruffing, she can then get back to dummy with a trump, discard a club and two diamonds on the hearts and concede a diamond to make four. However, the more aesthetic way to make four is to play the ace and finesse the jack of hearts! Now if the finesse loses, you are down one, but if it works you get rid of one club and three diamonds and still make four.

Ceci took the finesse ("West could have had four hearts, Edwin darling"). Naturally it worked, and naturally we got a good result.

Most of the pairs were in four going down one which Ceci was quick to point out to me as she gazed at the other scores on the pickup slip.

Ceci has recently given me another rule which states in no uncertain terms that we must bid any slam that makes. This, in turn, puts a little (just a little, mind you) pressure on me who, even without these ultimatums, has a tough enough time on slam hands. It turned out that Ceci and I missed a good seven hearts on these two hands, which cost us a Swiss Teams match.

WEST (Ceci)		EAST (Me)
♠ 4 2	N	♠ A Q 10 9 5
♡ A K 8 7 4 3	W E	♡ Q 6
◇ A K Q 6 5	S	◇ J 10
♣ —		♣ A Q 9 4

WEST	EAST
1♡	1♠
3◇	3♡
4♡	4NT
5♡	5NT
6♡	6NT
pass	

With the hearts breaking 3-2, there was no problem in the play. (It seemed to me that once Ceci knew that I had both black aces — when I bid 5NT, I promised all four aces held jointly — she might have bid the grand slam taking the slight gamble that I had the queen of hearts.) We had missed the grand slam and that was not so good. Then this one came up shortly thereafter:

WEST (Ceci)		EAST (Me)
♠ Q 5 4 3	N	♠ —
♡ A Q 10 6 5 4	W E	♡ J 9 2
◇ 5 4	S	◇ A K 7 3
♣ 3		♣ A K Q 8 4 2

WEST	NORTH	EAST	SOUTH
pass	pass	1♣	pass
1♡	1♠	2◇	pass
2♡	pass	2♠	pass
3♠!	pass	5♡	all pass

Making seven with the heart finesse onside. Well, this called for a little discussion. It turned out that my spade cuebid had confused her and her spade raise had scared her. That is why we did not reach this slam although we did agree that my jump to five was asking about the quality of her trump suit. So that was two slams down the tubes and even Minny (the Maltese, remember?) was getting restless watching this ineptness. Then came this number:

Vul: North-South
Dealer: East

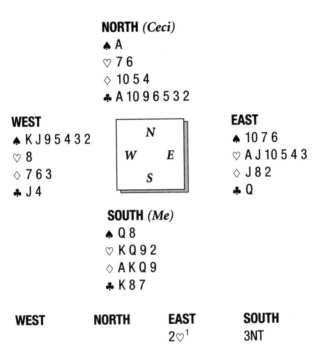

NORTH *(Ceci)*
♠ A
♡ 7 6
◇ 10 5 4
♣ A 10 9 6 5 3 2

WEST
♠ K J 9 5 4 3 2
♡ 8
◇ 7 6 3
♣ J 4

EAST
♠ 10 7 6
♡ A J 10 5 4 3
◇ J 8 2
♣ Q

SOUTH *(Me)*
♠ Q 8
♡ K Q 9 2
◇ A K Q 9
♣ K 8 7

WEST	NORTH	EAST	SOUTH
		2♡[1]	3NT

1. Weak

At this point, West asked Ceci what my 3NT bid meant. Ceci answered that it was forcing to game. West passed and Ceci leaped to six notrump, the only slam that makes. A heart ruff will beat any suit slam. But our very best hand was the following:

Vul: North-South
Dealer: West

WEST *(Me)*		EAST*(Ceci)*
♠ A K Q 7 6	N	♠ 5 3
♡ —	W E	♡ 7 6 3
◇ 6 5 3	S	◇ K J 4
♣ Q 8 7 6 4		♣ A K J 9 3

WEST	NORTH	EAST	SOUTH
1♠[1]	pass	2♣	pass
3♣	pass	3◇	pass
3♡	dbl	4♣	pass
6♣	all pass		

1. In my book I recommend opening these minimum 5-5 black hands with one club — but that book was written before I met Ceci and she has altered my bidding style somewhat

Before selecting a lead, South asked Ceci about the meaning of my three heart bid. Ceci's answer would have gladdened the heart of any partner. "Oh, he's either asking me or telling me something. I don't know, and I don't care."

A heart was led, Ceci ruffed, drew trumps in two rounds, and set up the spades (they were 4-2) for two diamond discards to make a slam with only twenty-three high card points between the combined hands.

Who knows, maybe I will get to third place one of these days.

And Then I Got Married

Unless one actually does it, one cannot understand the enormous psychological factors involved in being married to another bridge player. The urge to impress the love of your life is rather strong, if you know what I mean.

Early in my marriage (it would have to have been early as I was only married a little over a year) to Phyllis, we sauntered over to the plush Savoy Bridge Club in Los Angeles, where I immediately cut into the high-stake game. Phyllis kibitzed with watchful eyes, if you know what I mean.

It wasn't too long before this hand came up. Both sides were vulnerable and my partner, Kai Larsen, was the dealer:

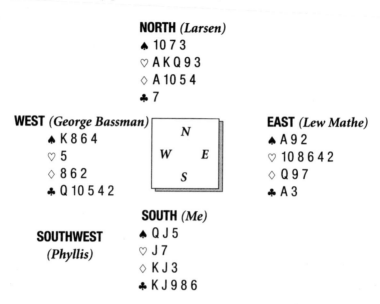

NORTH *(Larsen)*
♠ 10 7 3
♡ A K Q 9 3
◇ A 10 5 4
♣ 7

WEST *(George Bassman)*
♠ K 8 6 4
♡ 5
◇ 8 6 2
♣ Q 10 5 4 2

EAST *(Lew Mathe)*
♠ A 9 2
♡ 10 8 6 4 2
◇ Q 9 7
♣ A 3

SOUTH *(Me)*
♠ Q J 5
♡ J 7
◇ K J 3
♣ K J 9 8 6

SOUTHWEST
(Phyllis)

Kai opened one heart and I responded two notrump. I had to show Phyllis right off that I was no point-counter, and while others might need thirteen points to respond two notrump, I could get by with twelve. Kai rebid three diamonds and my confident three notrump ended the auction. George led the club four and I could hardly resist a sideways glance when I got this lead into oh-so-cleverly-concealed five-card suit.

Mathe, one of the club's owners, won the ace and after a moment of reflection, shifted to the spade deuce. I tried the queen, Bassman won the king and continued with the spade eight! I played low from dummy, Mathe played the spade nine and I won the jack. The hand did not appear to be difficult. It seemed I had oodles of tricks. I played the jack of hearts and a second heart. When Bassman discarded a club, my oodles had suddenly become eight.

Oh well, great players don't let bad breaks bother them. Besides, Phyllis was watching me, checking on my composure. Fortunately, she couldn't see my Southeast perspiration from her Southwest chair. Stalling, I played a third heart, discarding a club, while Bassman discarded a diamond.

It looked to me like George had started with five or six clubs, three spades, one heart and either three or four diamonds. For a great player, I have the curious habit of misguessing queens so, rather than take the diamond finesse one way or the other, I exited with a spade from dummy, cleverly unblocking their spade suit.

The possibility that Bassman had four spades, I admit, never crossed my mind. Who returns the spade eight from ♠K864? Mathe won the ace and took a little while to consider the position. He couldn't fool me, I 'knew' he was afraid to cash his fourth spade for fear of squeezing George in the minors. Who did he think he was playing against anyway?

As I suspected, he exited with a club. Don't worry Lew, I'm on to your game and Phyllis, are you watching? At this point I had the K-J-3 of diamonds and the K-J-9 of clubs and had lost three tricks. What could be sweeter? On Mathe's club shift, I would simply pass the club nine into Bassman's hand and wait for the minor-suit return which would insure my ninth trick.

I couldn't resist the grand gesture. When I played the club, I tabled my cards and announced, "George, you're endplayed for my ninth trick."

"By God, you're right," said George as he cashed the spade six for the setting trick.

Come to think of it, how did I stay married for so long?

Help!

Before I tell you about the following hand (played in a friendly, non-stake Team of Four game) you should be armed with a number of pertinent facts:

1. Marshall Miles is one of my very best friends.
2. He is usually a most discerning declarer, even though at times a little exotic.
3. He is addicted to making sensational leads if he feels the bidding calls for it.
4. He is often filled with admiration for an opponent who has hoodwinked him with a Miles-type zany brilliancy.
5. He stays over as a house guest whenever he comes in from San Bernardino for the weekend.
6. He and Phyllis (my wife) get along very well and recently had two nice sessions playing the Mixed Pairs at the Nationals in Denver.
7. He has a theory about rebidding five-card majors after partner's non-forcing one notrump response. Whenever Marshall has a broken two-loser suit such as KQ109x, AJ109x or KJ109x, he prefers to rebid the suit rather than pass with a minimum balanced hand. This, of course, is counter to standard practice.
8. Marshall, a bachelor, is hopelessly attracted to wild, imaginative women — particularly the married ones.

Keep all this in mind as I am going to ask you to help me answer an important question later. But first this hand:

Vul: Both
Dealer: South

NORTH
♠ 4
♡ K 10 6
♢ Q 10 6 5 4
♣ A 9 8 7

WEST *(Phyllis)*
♠ A 3 2
♡ 7 5 2
♢ K 9
♣ K J 6 5 4

```
        N
    W       E
        S
```

EAST *(Me)*
♠ Q 7 6 5
♡ Q 8 4 3
♢ J 3 2
♣ Q 10

SOUTH *(Marshall)*
♠ K J 10 9 8
♡ A J 9
♢ A 8 7
♣ 3 2

WEST	NORTH	EAST	SOUTH
			1♠
pass	1NT	pass	2♠[1]
all pass			

1. The theory in action

Phyllis, without a moment's hesitation, led the nine of diamonds! Marshall played dummy's ten and when I covered with the jack, Marshall for some obscure reason misread the diamond position. He thought that I had ◇KJx and Phyllis ◇9x. How naive! In any event, he ducked my jack in an effort to cut communications and avoid the impending diamond ruff. Slightly upended by this turn of events, I returned a diamond just to see what was going on. The diamond was ducked, and when Phyllis won the king there was a strange look in Marshall's eyes. He glanced to his left and gave Phyllis a long look. Was it hate or admiration?

At any rate, Phyllis returned her heart, covered by the ten, queen and ace. Marshall tried the king of spades which lost to the ace. He won the club return, entered his hand via a heart and sneakily played his eight of spades. I won the queen. When I turned up with the odd diamond and Phyllis ruffed Marshall's ace, my worst fears were confirmed...

Marshall was positively enthralled with that opening lead. He didn't even mind being the only player this side of the Atlantic not to take a diamond trick with this holding... nor did he mind going down a trick, the only pair in the room to achieve a minus score with the North-South cards.

Perhaps you have already guessed my question. In view of what I have told you about Marshall and in view of this opening lead, should I or should I not let him be our house guest next weekend?

Help!

Bridge at the Courthouse

◆

It came as a shock when Judy, my ex-girlfriend, told me she was going to be on jury duty for the next two weeks. Judy? Judy, who plays tennis and paddle-tennis every day of her life after work, would be locked up all day in City Hall? Impossible. She would never make it through the first day.

There was a chance she might make it, she said. They were given a two-hour lunch break. She would use that time to rush over to the paddle-tennis courts and get a few sets in. She would then put her 'jury clothes' over her tennis outfit and rush back. She might be able to survive, after all. I breathed easier, thinking how I would feel in the same position.

Later that week, Judy mentioned that while waiting to be empaneled she had actually rounded up a bridge game. Two of the women were duplicate players from the area, but the fourth was a little less sophisticated. In fact, that was the problem — trying to shape up that fourth. When playing with her, all jump bids were strong, all 4NT bids were Blackwood, all doubles were left in, and Stayman was not part of her vocabulary. What to do? They decided to teach her Stayman.

Judy was the first to feel the brunt of this lesson. The lady opened 2♣ with a 22-count and 4-4-2-3 distribution. When Judy responded 2♢, the lady rebid 3♣ to ask for a major. This led to a 5♣ contract, down five. The woman constantly blamed Judy during the play for their missed 4-4 heart fit.

Playing with the same woman the next day, Judy picked up the following hand, with neither side vulnerable.

♠ A K Q 10 9 8 7   ♡ 2   ◇ A K   ♣ A Q 10

She heard her right-hand opponent open 1♡. What to bid?

Double was out — she didn't want to defend 1♡ doubled with this hand. Science was out — besides, I always tell her that she is too timid. So she simply leapt to 6♠ (she was going to show me).

West led the ◇Q and this was the entire hand:

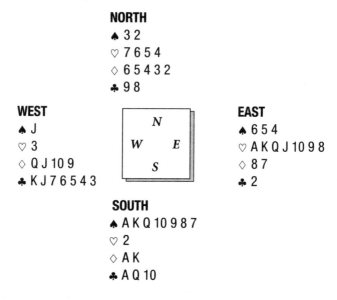

NORTH
♠ 3 2
♡ 7 6 5 4
◇ 6 5 4 3 2
♣ 9 8

WEST
♠ J
♡ 3
◇ Q J 10 9
♣ K J 7 6 5 4 3

EAST
♠ 6 5 4
♡ A K Q J 10 9 8
◇ 8 7
♣ 2

SOUTH
♠ A K Q 10 9 8 7
♡ 2
◇ A K
♣ A Q 10

You have to understand some of the emotions that were going on here. North had never heard such crazy bidding, nor had she ever wanted to. Why couldn't she have found a nice quiet game where the people didn't leap around so much or play funny conventions — Blackwood was enough.

Judy on the other hand was angry at me! She never would have bid 6♠ if I hadn't teased her over the years about her conservative nature. Now the lady was going to get angry again.

In her paranoia, Judy actually thought she saw a way to make the hand. If she could ruff a club she could discard her heart.

"On what?" I asked her.

"I don't know," she said. Shades of Yvonne (current girlfriend).

"So how did the play go?" I asked.

"Well, I won the diamond and played the ace and ten of clubs. West won the jack as East discarded her remaining diamond. West continued with the club king. I ruffed in dummy and East overruffed. I was so upset."

"You mean you couldn't get rid of your heart now?"

She gave me one of those looks that she saves just for me. "East then played two rounds of hearts and I was so mad at you I forgot to ruff high. West overruffed and returned a diamond which East ruffed. By the time I got around to drawing trumps, there weren't many left — down four."

It occurred to me that perhaps I should go down to the courthouse and see what was going on. After all, Judy had told me that the two duplicate players knew me, and the courthouse was very close to my home.

When I arrived with Yvonne a little before lunch, the game was in full swing. The women stopped playing, invited me into the game and offered Yvonne some donuts. But first they wanted to tell a Judy story. It seems that Judy sits on pins and needles every day hoping to be excused early (I never would have guessed). One day the husband of one of the women showed up to talk to his wife. Judy did not see him come in. Several minutes later when he started to leave, Judy stopped him.

"Hey," she said, "you can't go If you go, I want to go too."

On with the game. 'The lady', who had heard from the others that I was a pretty good player, was reluctant to play, so she sat at my side. Yvonne, who had finished all the donuts, was to be my partner. Judy would kibitz Yvonne.

This was our first and only hand:

Vul: East-West — hungry
Dealer: North — full

NORTH *(Yvonne)*
♠ K J 8 7
♡ A K 8 7
◇ A Q 9 8
♣ J

SOUTH *(Me)*
♠ A 10 6 5 3
♡ 2
◇ 10 7 4 2
♣ A Q 9

WEST	NORTH	EAST	SOUTH
	1◇	2♡	2♠
pass	3♡	pass	4◇
pass	6♠	all pass	

The jump to 6♠ came after a minor consultation with Judy.

Well, here I was at the Santa Monica courthouse with my kib-itzer watching my every move. The opening lead was the ♡6. What to do? Unless both diamond honors were on side, I would have to find the ♠Q. I decided that East, who was known to be long in hearts, should be short in spades. Accordingly, I won the opening lead and led a spade to the ace and a spade to the jack. It lost to the queen. 'The lady' got up to leave. She had seen enough. Didn't I even know the simplest of rules — eight ever, nine never? Even though I still made the hand (both diamond honors were right), she was not impressed. "He should have made seven."

Fortunately, Judy no longer has jury duty.

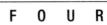
The Home
Game

My Home Game

Author's Note

I have written a number of 'Home Game' stories starring Yvonne Snyder as the heroine of some of the deals. This is a brief profile of a woman whom I regard highly and who has since become my wife.

Yvonne is the widowed mother of two sons. The elder, who is disabled, attended Stanford University. The younger graduated from the Berkeley College of Music.

Yvonne has done work with programs for the handicapped and she now splits her time between teaching Spanish in an adult education program and counseling parents of minority children. Seldom does one meet a person so loved and admired. All who know her feel that way. Another unusual trait she has is that she doesn't fear growing old. She doesn't try to cover up the years. Of course, having movie-star looks doesn't hurt.

She has a special relationship with her sons. When they talk, the trust between them is mutual and complete. So, really, how much does it matter if Yvonne has trouble counting a bridge hand (something she's actually learning to do)?

My few remaining fans may be wondering why they haven't seen my name in the winner's circle much in the past few years. After mulling the problem over, I have come up with at least two reasons (excuses) for my current demise:

1) My regular partner, Alan Sontag, lives in New York City, and we play together only three or four times a year.
2) The home game that I have been playing in regularly for the past five years.

Since Alan is a wonderful player, I can only conclude that it must be the home game. Let me tell you a little about the players and then show you a representative hand. The lineup:

Judy. Former girlfriend who is so thrilled that she got rid of me that she still has me over for dinner at least once a week. These dinners are followed by bridge. Judy is a ticket agent for American Airlines, and she currently gets up at 4:30 a.m. (This is relevant.)

Roy. Her husband, very bright and, if not the nicest guy in the world, must rank in the top ten on everybody's list. When Judy reflects on this, I sometimes get invited to dinner twice a week.

Yvonne. My girlfriend. Bilingual schoolteacher and mother of two. Yvonne used to enjoy bridge before she met me, before she was introduced to such awful terms as thinking, remembering, signaling and worst of all, counting.

I have tried to shape this game up (terrorize it) in a number of ways. I badger both Roy and Judy to be more aggressive in the bidding, and ask them questions during the play and defense to keep them thinking bridge. As for Yvonne, she has a tendency (compulsion) to overcall on moth-infested four-card suits. On the plus side, whenever she makes a penalty double, both Roy and Judy shiver.

At one time or another I have noticed each of the players heave a sigh of relief when they are dummy, knowing that the inquisition is over for the moment. The level of the game is actually improving (it had to), but then again, every so often something happens such as I am about to describe.

It might be helpful to tell you a bit about the previous hand. Judy had preempted in spades, and Yvonne became declarer in four clubs. Roy led the ace of spades. They play suit preference signals by the preemptor, and Judy, holding the ace of diamonds and a heart void, played the spade two, asking for a diamond (she should have signaled for a heart).

Roy shifted to a heart, Judy ruffed, underled her diamond ace to Roy's king and ruffed another heart. She then cashed the diamond ace to put us two down. They were happy with this result, but I couldn't bear to see all this glee go by without making a few cutting remarks. For openers, I did not tell them that they could make four

spades. I may be mean, but I am not cruel. Besides, Yvonne doesn't like it if I say anything sarcastic.

"Judy, why did you play the two of spades?"

"I had the ace of diamonds and wanted Roy to shift to a diamond."

"What about your heart void?"

"I forgot I was void in hearts; I got up very early this morning."

At this point Yvonne nodded in understanding. She also gets up early. Yvonne always understands and agrees with Judy's explanations — a soul sister, so to speak.

"Roy, why did you shift to a heart after partner asked you for a diamond?"

"Because I had five hearts, dummy had five and Judy hasn't had much sleep today."

With that as background, let's look at the hand of the evening. Let it be known that I have asked for written releases from the other players so I could write this hand up (none were given).

Vul: Both sides stuffed with a great dinner
Dealer: North

NORTH (*Me*)
♠ K 10 8 7
♡ 2
◇ J 8
♣ A Q J 10 3 2

WEST (*Roy*)
♠ 3
♡ A 9 8 7
◇ K Q 10 5 4
♣ 9 8 7

	N	
W		E
	S	

EAST (*Judy*)
♠ Q J 9 6 2
♡ K 10 6 3
◇ 3 2
♣ 5 4

SOUTH (*Yvonne*)
♠ A 5 4
♡ Q J 5 4
◇ A 9 7 6
♣ K 6

WEST	NORTH	EAST	SOUTH
	1♣	pass	1♡[1]
pass	1♠	pass	2NT
pass	3♣[2]	pass	3♡
pass	3NT	all pass	

1. Had her diamond ace in with her hearts. Had she seen the hand as it actually was, she probably would have responded 2NT. She saves this type of four-card suit for her overcalls
2. Prepared to tell Yvonne that three clubs was forcing if she passed and we missed game, or that three clubs was not forcing if she bid on and we went down. (My word has been law in this game — until this article appeared.)

Opening Lead: ◇K

As I began to put the dummy down, clubs and diamonds first, Yvonne, who never, ever says anything when she sees dummy, blurted out, "I don't believe this."

I couldn't figure out what she was talking about. She hadn't seen my major-suit cards, so how could she possibly know I was a little on the light side? It turned out, of course that she thought she had three little diamonds, and that I had bid notrump without a diamond stopper. She forgot she had bid notrump first.

Now for the play (?). The diamond king and queen both held, and Roy continued with the ten (!). Judy discarded the spade two, upside-down attitude (we all use the modern signaling methods), and Yvonne followed with the nine.

Roy was now caught on the horns of a dilemma that could only happen in this game. Was there no ace of diamonds in this deck? Was Yvonne holding up, holding up and holding up once again? Had Judy revoked? Was the ace of diamonds on the floor? I was in a game where not one of the four players knew who had the ace of diamonds.

Although the hand could now be defeated with a heart switch. Roy decided to play for the ace of diamonds to be on the floor and continued the suit. But Yvonne was ready for that play. As she was about to discard a heart rather than a spade, she discovered her ace of diamonds and quickly took her nine tricks. No big deal.

My question is: in this atmosphere, it's not possible that my game has slipped a bit, is it?

Bridge Alfresco

◆

It was a warm, sunny afternoon. Why not move the home game outdoors? By home game standards, the first deal was routine. Yvonne picked up:

♠ 8 7 5 4 3   ♡ 10 5 4   ◇ A K 9 8   ♣ 3

I opened 1♡ and she raised to 2♡, ending the auction. When she put down dummy however, she put down four low spades and two low clubs. This clever dummy placement had two effects: the opponents didn't see the urgency of leading trumps — and I took a practice finesse in clubs holding ♣AQ6 when I could have ruffed two clubs in dummy. I decided to put on my glasses for the next deal. I needed them. It was a distributional freak, and caused unusual vibrations.

Vul: Both   **Dealer:** South

NORTH *(Roy)*
♠ A K 4
♡ A
◇ Q 4
♣ A K 8 7 6 5 4

WEST *(Yvonne)*
♠ 2
♡ K J 10 8 3 2
◇ J 8 5
♣ Q 10 3

```
        N
   W        E
        S
```

EAST *(Me)*
♠ —
♡ Q 9 7 6 5 4
◇ A 10 7 6 3 2
♣ 9

SOUTH *(Judy)*
♠ Q J 10 9 8 7 6 5 3
♡ —
◇ K 9
♣ J 2

WEST	NORTH	EAST	SOUTH
			4♠
pass	4NT	5♡	?

My 5♡ bid caused Judy to gasp and cry, "Oh, dear!" while Yvonne nearly fell out of her chair. I inferred from Judy's distress that she and Roy didn't have a clue about how to deal with interference. It was lesson time. Rather than go into DOPI and DEPO, I decided to do what Ralph Katz did with me in San Francisco before we played our once-a-decade pairs game. Ralph said, "Let's play DEPO," Okay, if it was good enough for us it was going to be good enough for them. I explained the convention.

Yvonne wanted to know if the king of trumps should be counted. "Sure," I said "we'll all play Key Card DEPO."

Still no response from Judy, who was pondering her hand ever so seriously. I was getting a little edgy. Hadn't I just given the perfect explanation?

Yvonne picked up on this, and said, "Maybe she doesn't know if zero is an even or an odd number."

Yvonne was right. Finally Judy doubled and Roy bid 6♠. He sounded so confident that I bid 7◊. I could see Yvonne's eyes light up. She was preparing to give me the best preference at the seven-level anybody has ever been given. It wasn't to be. Judy bid 7♠, ending the tortured auction. Yvonne found the diamond lead and the play was over quickly. I waited for the post-mortem, sensing that this was an 'article deal'.

Yvonne was first. "I can't believe I never got to bid hearts. Judy ruined everything when she bid seven spades."

Finally, Judy spoke, "This was all your fault, Edwin. You didn't tell me how to answer DEPO with a void."

Roy, who never says anything, offered: "C'mon. Let's play the next hand."

This was it (hands rotated for convenience):

Vul: North-South irritated
Dealer: South

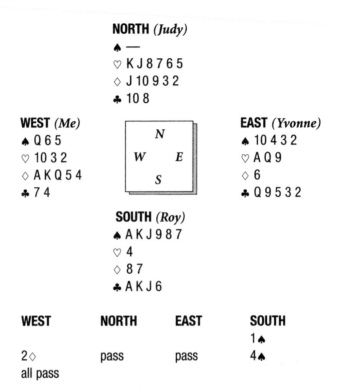

NORTH *(Judy)*
♠ —
♡ K J 8 7 6 5
♢ J 10 9 3 2
♣ 10 8

WEST *(Me)*
♠ Q 6 5
♡ 10 3 2
♢ A K Q 5 4
♣ 7 4

EAST *(Yvonne)*
♠ 10 4 3 2
♡ A Q 9
♢ 6
♣ Q 9 5 3 2

SOUTH *(Roy)*
♠ A K J 9 8 7
♡ 4
♢ 8 7
♣ A K J 6

WEST	NORTH	EAST	SOUTH
			1♠
2♢	pass	pass	4♠
all pass			

I led the ♢Q asking for count. Yvonne played her singleton ♢6. She said, "Are you looking under my card?" This was a reference to what I always tell my classes — when your partner plays a card, look *under* the card to see if any lower spot cards are missing.

"Yes, Yvonne, I am looking under your card."

I cashed a second diamond, on which Yvonne discarded the ♣5 — an upside-down discard. I shifted to the ♡2 and the jack went to Yvonne's queen. Yvonne shifted to a low club, won by dummy's ♣8. Roy continued with the ♣10, at which point I said, "Hope you haven't underled anything important."

"You didn't have to tell him did you?" Yvonne asked.

Roy took the second club finesse and eventually went down two after misguessing the spade position. An expected result. It's amazing how often, after all is said and done, we end up with more or less normal results. I couldn't resist asking Yvonne why, looking at an entryless dummy, she had shifted to a club. She said I had discarded a low club.

"I hadn't discarded anything," I said. "You discarded a club."

"I discarded a high club," she said, "or hadn't you noticed?"

"I noticed," I said.

"Besides," she said, now that she remembered why she had switched to a club, "you had led the ♡2, which looked like you wanted a club back."

Stay tuned.

Yvonne Makes her Little Diamond

◆

When we play the home game we keep score, but only the winning side adds it up. The other side isn't interested. One evening Yvonne and I were ahead by 1340 points with only one hand to go. Here it is:

Vul: Both
Dealer: West

NORTH (*Me*)
♠ 10 9 8 6
♡ A 4
◇ A 8 6
♣ A 7 3 2

WEST (*Roy*)
♠ A K Q 4
♡ J 10 9 8 5 2
◇ 7 4
♣ J

EAST (*Judy*)
♠ —
♡ K 7 3
◇ K Q 10 5 2
♣ Q 10 9 8 5

SOUTH (*Yvonne*)
♠ J 7 5 3 2
♡ Q 6
◇ J 9 3
♣ K 6 4

WEST	NORTH	EAST	SOUTH
1♡	dbl	4♡	4♠
dbl	all pass		

Opening Lead: ♡J

Judy made a tactical raise to game and Yvonne, not wanting to be labeled a wimp, plunged right in with 4♠. Roy knew what to do with that bid. Judy won the opening lead and shifted to a tricky ◊Q.

(I wanted Roy to play the jack if he had it, but I knew that he wouldn't. My God, I've created a monster.)

Yvonne ducked. Back came a club to the ace followed by the ♡A. That was two tricks for us. (I was beginning to count.)

A spade went to Roy's queen and back came a diamond which was ducked again! Roy ruffed the diamond return, cashed his high spades, but was forced to lead a heart. Dummy ruffed this and the losing club was pitched. Down four — *only* 1100. We had held on.

Yvonne, who had never gone down 1100 in her life, was numb. What to say?

"Good play cashing that ace of hearts, otherwise you would have lost a club trick as well." Silence.

Finally she spoke. "That was a lousy double."

Before going into the 'key' hand of our next encounter, let me digress a moment. Yvonne was in Reno for a few days for the Spring NABC. I noticed that Mike Lawrence was giving a lecture on splinter bids and mentioned that perhaps she should attend.

"Why should I go?" she asked. "I have never used one yet." I told her that they aren't complicated — they are simply jump bids made with a fit, one level higher than a jump shift. "So what will he talk about for an hour?"

Yvonne also helps me with my classes when she is not working. She fills in when needed. Recently, during a lesson on third-hand play, I posed this situation to the class:

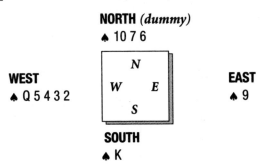

NORTH (*dummy*)
♠ 10 7 6

WEST
♠ Q 5 4 3 2

EAST
♠ 9

SOUTH
♠ K

The idea was for each student to pretend that he or she was West and had led a low spade against a notrump contract. Dummy had played low, partner had played the nine and declarer had won with the king. Now came the questions.

"Who has the ace? Who has the jack?" After most of them had fielded those, I asked somewhat smugly, "And who has the eight?"

"Who cares?" was the most popular answer to that one.

After the class I asked Yvonne, if she had figured out who had the ♠8. "No," she said, "I only go down as far as the jack myself."

The key hand of our next set game also stars Yvonne sitting East. The victim was poor Roy in the South seat. Judy was dummy and I was West:

Vul: Both
Dealer: South

NORTH *(Judy)*
♠ Q 4
♡ K J 8 7 6 4
◇ A 10 5
♣ 6 2

WEST *(Me)*
♠ A J 10 9 5
♡ Q
◇ Q 9 6 3
♣ K 9 8

	N	
W		E
	S	

EAST *(Yvonne)*
♠ 7 3 2
♡ 10 5 3 2
◇ K 8 7 2
♣ Q 7

SOUTH *(Roy)*
♠ K 8 6
♡ A 9
◇ J 4
♣ A J 10 5 4 3

WEST	NORTH	EAST	SOUTH
			1♣
1♠	2♡	pass	3♣
pass	3♠	pass	3NT
all pass			

Opening Lead: ♠10 (0 or 2 higher)

When Judy put the dummy down she asked me about her 3♠
bid. I usually like to answer these questions after the deal so I can
see what happens first, but this time she nailed me early.

"It looks good to me," I said. Roy won the opening lead in
dummy, Yvonne playing an impeccable deuce — count. At Trick 2
Roy led a club to the jack which held. Roy shifted his attack to
hearts, cashing the ♡A and playing a second heart to the king as I
shed a low diamond. Yvonne high-lowed giving me count. Some of
these lessons were paying off after all.

Roy by now had an *idée fixe*, as the French say, that Yvonne had
both club honors. Apparently in this game I have never ducked a
trick that I could have won. In any case, Roy exited with a low diamond from dummy! In spite of the fact that I had signaled weak-
ness in diamonds, Yvonne ducked. I won and exited with a diamond
to the ten and the king. Yvonne now played another diamond!

Roy was now 100% convinced that Yvonne had no more spades.
He decided that Yvonne's original distribution had been 1-4-4-4, so
he discarded a spade on the ◊A. Next, he led a club off dummy and
ducked Yvonne's queen. If his assumptions were correct, Yvonne
would cash a fourth diamond upon which he would discard the ♠K,
and then Yvonne would have to return either a club in which case his
hand was high, or a heart in which case dummy was high.
Impressive.

Sure enough, Yvonne cashed her diamond, but then, lo and
behold, she produced a spade and I claimed! Down five! Once
again, silence around the table. Finally Roy turned to Yvonne and
said, "I didn't think you had any more spades. I was having trouble
counting the hand." (No wonder.)

Yvonne now came to life. "I knew you had spades, Eddie, I did.
Besides, we beat it five tricks, and didn't you see me make my little
diamond?"

Judy piped up, "Let's go on to the next hand before we all wind
up in an article."

Too late, Judy, too late.

Claim Jumper

◆

The home game has been progressing more or less serenely these days, but it has been noticed that the play is somewhat slow. Seldom does the home game finish more than three or four Chicago rubbers (four deals each) in two hours.

In order to speed up the game, claiming has been encouraged. The accuracy of the claims varies with a plus ratio of 70% to 80% and about a 1.2-trick spread in what can be made and what the claimer announces can be made. These figures did not factor in the following deal:

Vul: Both   **Dealer:** North

NORTH
- ♠ J 7 6 4
- ♡ Q
- ◊ A K
- ♣ A K 9 7 4 2

```
        N
   W         E
        S
```

SOUTH *(Yvonne)*
- ♠ 3
- ♡ A K J 5
- ◊ Q J 7 4 2
- ♣ 6 5 3

WEST	NORTH	EAST	SOUTH
	1♣	pass	1◊
pass	1♠	pass	2NT
pass	3NT	all pass	

West led the ♡9. Yvonne took a cursory look at dummy and in the interest of 'speeding up the game', immediately claimed eleven tricks: five diamonds, four hearts and two clubs. Blocked suits and entry problems are sometimes subordinated to the greater good of getting on with the game.

What should I do if no one notices that this claim had broken all previous records for false home-game claims? I didn't have to worry, both Roy and Judy saw at a glance that there might be a little trouble realizing all of those red-suit winners and so announced.

In Yvonne's defense, she said later she thought she saw two hearts in the dummy. Well, before I tell you what happened, let's make this a Test Your Home Game Play in two parts:

1) How should Yvonne play the actual deal?
2) How should Yvonne play if the diamonds in the closed hand are Q-J-10-3-2 instead of Q-J-7-4-2?

Solutions

1) Allow the ♡Q to hold and play the ♣A and ♣K. If clubs break 2-2, cash the ◇A and ◇K, cross to the closed hand with a club and take your red-suit winners. If diamonds behave, you wind up with twelve tricks.

If clubs are 3-1, cash the ◇A and ◇K and exit dummy with a club. If the opponents' spades are blocked (why shouldn't spades be blocked along with hearts and diamonds?) and the opponents cannot take four spade tricks, you still wind up making your contract.

2) Overtake the opening lead, play off two more top hearts, discarding dummy's high diamonds, and play your high diamonds. If diamonds break 3-3, you wind up taking either ten tricks or thirteen tricks depending upon how clubs divide. If diamonds don't break 3-3, you need a 2-2 club division.

What happened

Stuck in the dummy at Trick 1, Yvonne cashed the ♣A and ♣K. When clubs divided 2-2, she cashed the ◇K, crossed to her hand with a club, and wound up taking twelve tricks. "What's all this fuss about" asked Yvonne. "I only claimed eleven tricks. Wasn't that good enough? I thought we were trying to save time."

Cross Ruff

A few years ago, I endured one of the more humiliating experiences of my bridge career. It all started with a telephone call from Ron Andersen.

"Edwin, I am involved with a new bridge promotion called 'Cross Ruff'. Twelve pre-dealt lesson hands together with sealed hand analyses are included in each set. More lesson hands may be needed. Will you take a look?"

"Sure, Ron." A few weeks later, in came two sets of 'Cross Ruff'. One was labeled for beginners, the other for intermediates.

The 'trial' would be a very informal dinner-bridge party. There were six of us, four of whom I would classify as intermediate players. Yvonne, my girlfriend, was partnered by Shar, the hostess. The other two players were my good friends from the home game, Roy and Judy. In addition, I was sitting next to Yvonne as sort of a coach-explainer and Shar's friend Marshall, a good player, was sitting next to her as a consultant. The first few deals were interesting and everybody seemed to get the main points

This was the fourth deal. Yvonne, East, picked up, both sides vulnerable:

♠ A 7 6 5   ♡ 5   ◇ A 10 8 3 2   ♣ 9 8 5

MARSHALL/SHAR	JUDY	YVONNE/ME	ROY
			1♡
pass	2NT[1]	pass	3♣
pass	4♡	pass	4NT[2]
pass	5♣[3]	pass	5♡
all pass			

1. Could be balanced heart raise if followed by 4♡
2. Roman Key Card
3. 1 or 4 (I have them trained)

Shar had an opening lead all ready when Marshall objected, "Not with a balanced hand." Finally, after much hemming and hawing, the ◇9 hit the table. Down showered the dummy:

NORTH *(dummy)*
♠ Q J 10 9
♡ K 10 7 6
◇ K Q J
♣ J 2

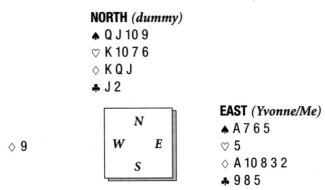

◇ 9

EAST *(Yvonne/Me)*
♠ A 7 6 5
♡ 5
◇ A 10 8 3 2
♣ 9 8 5

'We' won the ◇A and I began to think. Could this lead possibly be a singleton?

(1) That would give Roy 0-5-4-4 distribution and it is unlikely he would use RKCB with a void. In addition, Marshall had already mentioned that the lead was being made from a balanced hand. Perhaps Roy was 1-6-2-4, 1-6-1-5 or 1-5-2-5. In those cases, I had to cash the ♠A and hope partner had the ♣K or perhaps ♡Qxx. Maybe Roy was 2-5-2-4 without the ♠K. Again, our side had to cash two fast spade tricks. However, if Roy was 3-5-1-4, 2-5-2-4 or 1-5-3-4 with the ♠K, it was necessary to shift to a club before the clubs went off on the spades and diamonds.

Everybody was looking at me. After all, this *was* an intermediate hand, wasn't it? Why was I taking so long? I was supposed to be the expert here. The others had all made their 'key' plays faster than this. I was still troubled by all of the patterns that I had assigned to Roy that contained a singleton diamond. Would Marshall have allowed Shar to lead the ◇9 from ◇9xxx? Finally I plunked down the ♠A — deuce from partner and Roy followed small. Two new thoughts crept in. Marshall's comment about a balanced hand notwithstanding, the lead could not have been a singleton because Roy would not have room in his hand for a spade. Also, because this is an attitude situation, partner could not have ♠Kxx; he would have played his middle spade. Maybe partner had ♠K2.

Was there any reason not to play a second spade? I could see myself basking in the glory of the hand analyses: "In spite of the fact that partner has played the discouraging ♠2, you only chance is to hope the deuce is from K-x."

So why did I have this uneasy feeling about this hand? Again, they were all looking at me. What was taking me so long? These were intermediate hands. I began to get warm under the collar. I didn't want to look bad, but I didn't know what to do. Maybe they had inadvertently stuck an advanced hand into the set and this was it. I couldn't stall any longer. I played a second spade. Roy ruffed, drew trumps and claimed. This was the entire deal:

NORTH
♠ Q J 10 9
♡ K 10 7 6
◇ K Q J
♣ J 2

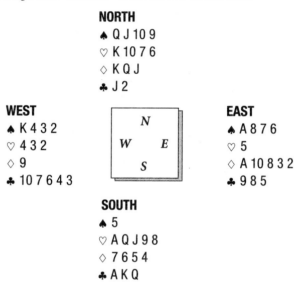

WEST
♠ K 4 3 2
♡ 4 3 2
◇ 9
♣ 10 7 6 4 3

EAST
♠ A 8 7 6
♡ 5
◇ A 10 8 3 2
♣ 9 8 5

SOUTH
♠ 5
♡ A Q J 9 8
◇ 7 6 5 4
♣ A K Q

The par was to beat four hearts (I couldn't beat five!). The idea, of course, was to win the diamond and return the ◇10, asking for a spade return after partner ruffs. The second diamond ruff defeats four hearts one trick. Not only did I fail to find the right defense, I also failed to recognize a hand that I use in my own class when I lecture on defensive signaling.

Not that I am looking for compassion (sure) but I would like to list the series of events that took place for me to blow a defense that

Ron had (quite correctly) classified as 'intermediate'.

1) The contract was five hearts, not four hearts. Everyone knows that it is easier to defeat four hearts than five hearts.
2) Roy had to bid a three-card suit and follow up with RKCB.
3) Marshall wouldn't let Shar make the obvious diamond lead.
4) Marshall told Shar 'not with a balanced hand'. How was I to know he meant not *against* a balanced hand — referring to the dummy?
5) Ten eyes were boring down upon me during the entire defense.

Marshall apologized, saying he should have dumped the ♠K under the ♠A to help me out.

"Why," chirped in Yvonne, "I would have returned a diamond right away. I don't even know what you were thinking about so long."

Anyway, thanks a ton, Ron, for sending me the hands. Everybody else had a wonderful evening.

A New Low

Whenever we play in our home game, I always urge Judy and Roy to be more aggressive — to bid their games and slams. But it seems that the harder I try, the more conservative they become. Near the end of one evening, we had a little excitement:

Vul: Neither
Dealer: East

NORTH *(Judy)*
♠ A Q 9 8 7 6
♡ 8
◇ —
♣ A K 10 4 3 2

WEST *(Yvonne)*
♠ 4 3
♡ K 10 7 2
◇ A K 3 2
♣ 8 6 5

EAST *(Me)*
♠ K 2
♡ A 9 6 3
◇ Q 10 9 7
♣ Q J 9

SOUTH *(Roy)*
♠ J 10 5
♡ Q J 5 4
◇ J 8 6 5 4
♣ 7

WEST	NORTH	EAST	SOUTH
		1◇	pass
1♡	2♡	dbl	2♠
3◇	4♠	pass	pass
dbl	all pass		

Good defense held this to five. Translation: we didn't lose our two sure tricks. Lesson time.

"Yvonne, when an opponent shows a two-suiter, you should not double when all of your strength is in our suits. You need tricks in their suits."

"Oh, I didn't know that. That makes sense," she said.

Well, I thought, I got that point across anyway.

A few deals later (hand rotated for convenience):

Vul: Both
Dealer: South

NORTH *(Roy)*
♠ 9 6 3
♡ 10 9 6 5
◇ K 5 4
♣ Q 6 4

WEST *(Me)*
♠ Q 10 4
♡ Q 2
◇ Q J 8 7
♣ K 10 8 7

```
      N
  W       E
      S
```

EAST *(Yvonne)*
♠ A K J 8 7 5
♡ —
◇ 10 9
♣ J 9 5 3 2

SOUTH *(Judy)*
♠ 2
♡ A K J 8 7 4 3
◇ A 6 3 2
♣ A

WEST	NORTH	EAST	SOUTH
			1♡
pass	2♡	3♡	4♡
4♠	pass	pass	5♡
dbl	all pass		

I led a low spade and Judy ruffed the second spade, remarking, "Edwin, when your partner shows a two-suiter you should have tricks outside of her suits to make a penalty double."

With that, she claimed.

I heard myself explaining, "Well, I only had three spades, I expected a slightly different hand from Yvonne — and remember, I didn't double 4♡, so I couldn't have a real stack."

Then I sank to a record low. I suggested that Yvonne might have removed my double to 5♠. I forgot that Yvonne does not remove penalty doubles. This comes from remembering what her own penalty doubles look like. When Yvonne doubles the opponents, declarer never goes down only one trick. Never.

Yvonne thought, she said, that I had some red-suit defensive tricks. After all, hadn't I just told her what one needs to double after a two-suited cuebid?

The Expert and the Rabbit

After a few encouraging sessions of bridge in which the level had risen to mediocre, the Home Game ran into some choppy waters. It all started when Yvonne opened 1NT with this hand:

♠ K Q 5   ♡ 10 3   ◇ A 9 8 5   ♣ A Q 7 6

Ostensibly, this looks O.K., playing a 15-17 notrump range. Actually, it would have been O.K. but this was Yvonne's actual hand, vulnerable versus not:

♠ K Q 5   ♡ —   ◇ A 10 9 8 5 3   ♣ A Q 7 6

As might be expected, the bidding took a somewhat slanted turn:

WEST	NORTH	EAST	SOUTH
Judy	Me	Roy	Yvonne
			1NT
2♡	2NT	pass	3◇[1]
pass	3NT[2]	all pass	

1. Recognizing that notrump might not be the best strain in view of the most recent sorting developments
2. A touching degree of faith

The opening lead was the ◇Q and this is what greeted Yvonne:

NORTH
♠ J 9 7
♡ K 7 3 2
◇ K Q 2
♣ 10 9 5

SOUTH *(Yvonne)*
♠ K Q 5
♡ —
◇ A 10 9 8 5 3
♣ A Q 7 6

Yvonne ducked the opening lead discarding a club. When Judy continued with the ♡J, Yvonne ducked again. Roy, mistakenly as it turned out, went up with the ace (Yvonne discarding a spade.) and continued with the ♡9. Judy overtook with the ten. Think about how you would proceed.

The hand presented no problem for Yvonne — discarding a second club, she attacked spades. As Roy had the ace and no more hearts, nine tricks came rolling in. Judy had the ♣KJx so five diamonds couldn't make. Was this the second coming of the Rueful Rabbit?

On the next hand the spotlight was on me. With both sides vulnerable I found myself looking at:

♠ — ♡ A J 6 4 ◇ 8 6 4 3 ♣ K Q 8 4 3

The bidding proceeded as follows:

WEST	NORTH	EAST	SOUTH
Judy	*Me*	*Roy*	*Yvonne*
1◇	pass	2◇	2♠
pass	?		

I reasoned that Yvonne must have at least six spades. Judy

couldn't have five spades and open 1♦ and Roy couldn't have four spades and raise to 2♦. Thus, I convinced myself to pass. The opening lead was a high diamond and this is what my 'reasoning' produced:

NORTH
♠ —
♡ A J 6 4
♢ 8 6 4 3
♣ K Q 8 4 3

SOUTH *(Yvonne)*
♠ A J 9 7 3
♡ K 2
♢ 10
♣ A J 9 6 5

Beautiful. We are practically a shoo-in for six clubs and I leave Yvonne playing two spades! Is it really possible to concentrate on making a contract of 2♠ with a diamond lead and diamond continuation when you see that ten-card club fit?

I think that Yvonne gave it her best shot. She ruffed the diamond continuation and played the heart king and a heart to the jack. If that holds, she can cash the ♡A, ruff a diamond, enter dummy with a club and ruff the appropriate red card from dummy. That plus the ♠A comes to eight tricks. Alas, it wasn't to be. Roy had the ♡Q and they defended well from that point on and Yvonne wound up with six tricks.

I was right about the distribution, though. Judy didn't have five spades and Roy didn't have four spades: Roy had *five* spades. This was the entire fateful deal:

NORTH *(Me)*
♠ —
♡ A J 6 4
♦ 8 6 4 3
♣ K Q 8 4 3

WEST *(Judy)*
♠ K 10 2
♡ 10 9 3
♦ A K Q 5 2
♣ 10 2

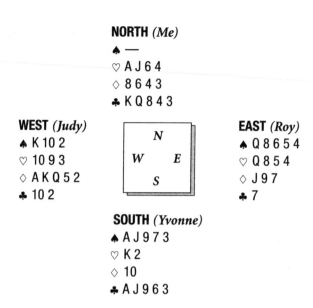

EAST *(Roy)*
♠ Q 8 6 5 4
♡ Q 8 5 4
♦ J 9 7
♣ 7

SOUTH *(Yvonne)*
♠ A J 9 7 3
♡ K 2
♦ 10
♣ A J 9 6 3

After the hand, Yvonne asked if 6♣ makes. What do you think? Assume that Judy leads a trump and persists with a second trump upon regaining the lead by ruffing a diamond.

The answer is yes, and there are many variations. Say Yvonne wins the trump lead in her hand, ruffs a low spade and exits a dia-

mond. Judy wins and plays a second trump, Roy discarding a diamond to prevent Yvonne from setting up a long card in either major. Assume that the second trump play is won in dummy and a diamond is ruffed in the closed hand followed by a second low spade ruff in dummy. Now a third diamond is led from dummy in this position:

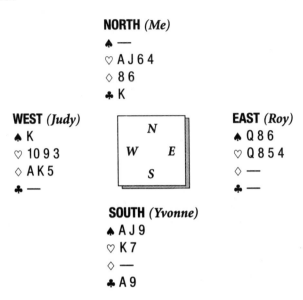

NORTH *(Me)*
♠ —
♡ A J 6 4
◇ 8 6
♣ K

WEST *(Judy)*
♠ K
♡ 10 9 3
◇ A K 5
♣ —

N
W   E
S

EAST *(Roy)*
♠ Q 8 6
♡ Q 8 5 4
◇ —
♣ —

SOUTH *(Yvonne)*
♠ A J 9
♡ K 7
◇ —
♣ A 9

Roy is squeezed. A discard in either suit allows declarer to set up that suit for her twelfth trick.

Nice pass, Eddie.

When Bad Things Happen

A Record, I Think

I teach my beginners that if both hands are balanced they should be in three notrump if they have 25-32 points. I tell them that even though most books say that they need twenty-six, after I am through teaching them how to play the hand, they will be able to make three notrump with at least one point less.

Getting back to the real world, we have all seen 3NT contracts come home with twenty-two or so combined points if there is a long suit, or if one opponent has too many high cards and must make some critical discards. On the other side of the ledger there are those 4333 hands that face each other with the defenders mockingly resisting every effort the declarer makes to bring in nine tricks despite a combined count of 27-28 high-card points.

My own personal record, and one I have not bragged about too often, is going down in three notrump with twenty-nine points between the two hands and no unstopped suit. It wasn't easy, you understand, but after a couple of finesses lost, and a couple of other suits didn't break, and I misread the end position, I managed to wind up with only eight. This happened seventeen years ago, and until the following deal I felt secure that twenty-nine would be my limit.

Playing in friendly rubber game not long ago, I dealt myself and the table this layout:

Vul: Both
Dealer: South

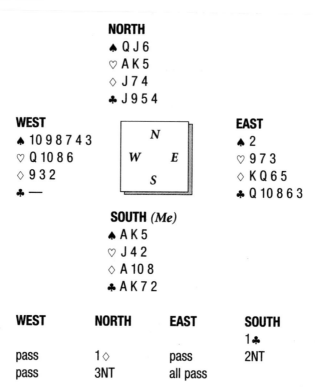

NORTH
♠ Q J 6
♡ A K 5
◇ J 7 4
♣ J 9 5 4

WEST
♠ 10 9 8 7 4 3
♡ Q 10 8 6
◇ 9 3 2
♣ —

EAST
♠ 2
♡ 9 7 3
◇ K Q 6 5
♣ Q 10 8 6 3

SOUTH (*Me*)
♠ A K 5
♡ J 4 2
◇ A 10 8
♣ A K 7 2

WEST	NORTH	EAST	SOUTH
			1♣
pass	1◇	pass	2NT
pass	3NT	all pass	

Opening Lead: ♠10

My partner, who had witnessed some of my previous notrump adventures over the years, cautiously raised me to game with his balanced twelve. Quickly and confidently, I won the spade in my hand and led the king of clubs. When West discarded a spade, the play slowed down to such an extent that my partner finally asked me if I was all right.

In fact, I was in a mild state of shock. Knowing that I now had only eight sure tricks, instead of being able to think about the best way to secure nine, all I could think was: "Kantar, you have thirty-one points between these two hands. For God's sake, figure something out or you will never live this one down."

Ever so daintily I crossed to the heart king and led a low diamond. East played the six. Still on top of my game, I stuck in the eight, knowing, just knowing that the nine would appear. It did. West got out with a spade and East discarded a heart (he should have thrown a club) and I won on the table.

Could this really be happening to a great player like me? At least, I had formulated a plan (I was going to have to tell my partner something after this hand was over). If I could somehow strip East of his red cards I could duck a club and force East to lead away from his queen of clubs; then this hand would just go down as another tough struggle — but not too tough. (Fifteen minutes had already elapsed.) I led a second diamond from the table and ducked East's queen. East returned a heart and once again, I realized I had a problem. This was the actual end position, just one card removed from what I thought it was:

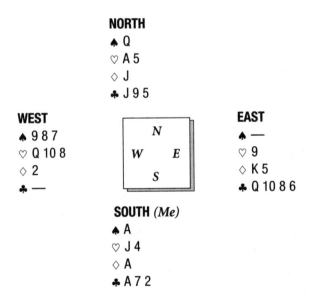

```
                    NORTH
                    ♠ Q
                    ♡ A 5
                    ◇ J
                    ♣ J 9 5

     WEST              ┌─────────┐       EAST
     ♠ 9 8 7           │    N    │       ♠ —
     ♡ Q 10 8          │ W     E │       ♡ 9
     ◇ 2               │    S    │       ◇ K 5
     ♣ —               └─────────┘       ♣ Q 10 8 6

                    SOUTH (Me)
                    ♠ A
                    ♡ J 4
                    ◇ A
                    ♣ A 7 2
```

In the actual position I can win the ace of hearts, cash my diamond and spade winners, and toss East in with a low club. East cashes a diamond, upon which I throw losing hearts from both hands, but is finally forced to lead away from that queen of clubs for my ninth trick. However, I thought that East had one more heart and one less diamond. If that is the case I cannot win the ace of hearts and cash a spade because East will then have a heart to get to West's spades.

If my idea was right, I could make the hand thus: duck the heart, win any return, cash my spade, heart and diamond winners, and then duck a club. Furthermore, if I was wrong and the cards were as they actually were, West would have to win the heart return and play specifically a diamond—or else I would still make the hand on a funny squeeze.

To make a long story a bit sadder, I ducked the heart and West shifted to a diamond. Now there was no way. I was finished. Down one worth thirty-one points between the two hands. Did I have a new record? I would have to wait until Guinness's next book came out. In the meantime I am advising my classes that they must have at least twenty-seven high-card points between the two hands to have a fairly good chance at three notrump.

Drawing Trumps — An Idea Worth Some Thought

To be a good bridge player you must be technically sound — but you must be psychologically sound as well. The latter is known as 'reading the position', or knowing something the cards don't actually tell you. Knowing what's going on is another way to put it. Along with others, I like to think that I can read my opponents — their mannerisms as well as their telltale hesitations. Once sniffed out they can be put to good use during the play of the hand.

Not long ago, my good friend John Szeps and I were looking for some tough competition, so we decided to play duplicate in the mighty side game at a Torrance Sectional. I told John to fill out the convention card. Whatever he put down would be our system for the evening. He returned his scratch marks to me and I noticed we were playing strong two-bids. Strong two-bids? Oh well, I thought, they never come up, so what if I don't remember the responses. One came up and we survived it, but the experience was so unnerving that John suggested that we go back to Weak Twos and Flannery. "Fine," I said, feeling a little more at home. But I did hear John muttering under his breath, "I hate Flannery."

Things were going along fine (no revokes) until the next-to-last round when I picked up, red against white, this motley collection:

♠ Q 8   ♡ 87   ◇ A J 4   ♣ Q 9 7 6 3 2

I heard John open 2◇ in the North seat. I alerted. My right-hand opponent, PhyLLiS Cook (with two Ls and one S — I learned the spelling when married to my first wife), asked about the bid, received an explanation and passed. I tried 2♡ which ended the auction. PhyLLiS passed slowly and John once again muttered under his breath, "but I hate Flannery."

My left hand opponent, Audrey Ellis of Manhattan Beach, led the ♣K at which time John asked if he was allowed to bid over 2♡. I said it would be unusual, but would he please expose the dummy so I could see what was bothering him so much. Finally he produced:

♠ A 6 3 2   ♡ A J 10 3 2   ◇ K Q 6   ♣ 4

I told him he had done just fine, that his hand wasn't worth another bid. He nodded, but I knew that in his heart he still wanted to bid again. And now, on to the play — the memorable play:

NORTH (*Disgruntled John*)
♠ A 6 3 2
♡ A J 10 3 2
◇ K Q 6
♣ 4

WEST (*Audrey*) 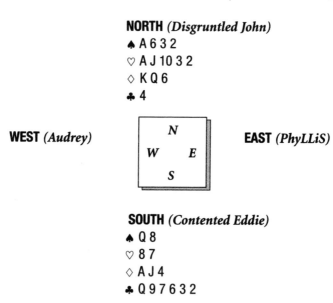 **EAST** (*PhyLLiS*)

SOUTH (*Contented Eddie*)
♠ Q 8
♡ 8 7
◇ A J 4
♣ Q 9 7 6 3 2

At Trick 2 Audrey shifted to the ◇10. I decided to win this in dummy and lead a low spade — a play which met with universal approval from the players (two) to whom I dared show the hand afterward. What followed can hardly be described. PhyLLiS won the ♠K and Audrey discarded a club. Very well, I thought, if they want to revoke, let them.

A spade came back and Audrey ruffed. Next a diamond. PhyLLiS ruffed and led another spade. I decided to discard my ◇A

— a big play in a side game— and Audrey ruffed. Without hesitation she played a third diamond which PhyLLiS ruffed with the nine — of course. A fourth spade was returned and ruffed by Audrey with the king. She then played a fourth diamond allowing East (I won't write that name again) to make her now blank ♡Q.

At this point both opponents cheerfully conceded ("I don't have any more trumps!" — "Neither do I") the rest of the tricks to dummy's ♡AJ103. (I had to ruff the fourth diamond in dummy, under East's ♡Q, because North was down to all trumps at that point.) It was time to assess the debacle, but very difficult as everybody at the table was laughing hilariously. Except South. I mentally noted the following:

1) I had managed to take exactly five tricks.
2) Trumps were 3-3 with the honors divided. Nevertheless, I had managed to lose six trump tricks!
3) Had I ruffed the third spade with the ♡7, I would have saved two tricks (but that is a losing play if West has the ♡9).
4) I had probably set a record which I should submit to the *Guinness Book of World Records* for the most trump tricks lost in a partscore contract.
5) Drawing trumps immediately is a technique I should consider more carefully in the future.

Down Seven, Redoubled

Speaking of records. On the first day of regular play at the Summer Nationals in Boston a few years ago, one pair achieved a score of plus 3070 on a single deal. The following day, the *Daily Bulletin* came out with the prediction that plus or minus 3070 would certainly be the biggest score any one pair would make on any one deal during the entire tournament. What the *Bulletin* overlooked was that the following day the Mixed Pairs was to be held. No logical predictions can be made until that event is over.

Vul: North-South
Dealer: East

NORTH
♠ 9 8 4 2
♡ 8 3 2
◇ J 7 6
♣ A Q 2

WEST
♠ 6
♡ K J 10 9 5
◇ 9 5 3
♣ J 8 7 3

EAST
♠ A K J 7 5
♡ 7
◇ A K Q 10 8 4 2
♣ —

SOUTH
♠ Q 10 3
♡ A Q 6 4
◇ —
♣ K 10 9 6 5 4

East opened with a forcing club and South conceived the bid of two diamonds! Surely, this overcall would produce some fireworks. West bid a peaceful two hearts, but when North raised to three diamonds, East chanced a double. South promptly redoubled for rescue but North didn't get the message and passed! East decided that three diamonds redoubled suited him fine so he passed also. West led his singleton spade.

Now for some good news and some bad news. The good news was that the defenders failed to find their spade ruff. The bad news was that even with this gift declarer went down seven tricks for a loss of 4000 points. More good news and bad news. The good news: North-South set a new minus record that did hold up for the remainder of the tournament. The bad news: neither North nor South seemed to appreciate what they had accomplished.

Partnerships have been known to break up over a single hand — even one bid or one errant play can do the trick. The next hand is an example of this in action, and I'm involved. Playing with my frequent partner, Marshall Miles, is at times trying. For example, he has devised a 'super method' for responding to a two notrump opening bid. The method is so complicated that bridge-playing math professors at both UCLA and USC have thrown up their hands in despair when the method was explained.

But I am expected to play it, come what may. Just to give you an insight into this method, a raise to three notrump is a transfer to four clubs.

In any event, we were using this method at a National Championships in Lancaster, Pennsylvania.

Fortunately, both Marshall and I are poor card-holders so neither one of us opened two notrump until he hung one on me on the last day of a ten-day tournament. By that time, I couldn't even remember the normal responses to two notrump let alone the all-encompassing Milesian responses. In any case, this was the hand that proved, beyond a shadow of a doubt, that honesty is always the best policy:

Vul: Both
Dealer: South

NORTH *(Me)*
♠ Q 4
♡ 7 6
◇ A J 10 7 6 3 2
♣ 5 4

SOUTH *(The Master)*
♠ A K 9 3
♡ A K 4
◇ K 8 5
♣ K 7 3

Marshall opened two notrump with the South cards, never once looking up to see whether or not I was going to remember the responses. Using 'the method' my proper response, the Master informed me later, was four diamonds — a slam try in diamonds. Well, who would have thought that diamonds meant diamonds? That bid never even entered my mind.

I naively thought that slam was remote and our best chance for a good tournament score was to play in three notrump. So I bid it! Keep in mind that the Master now thinks I have made a transfer to clubs, a slam try.

East passed and Marshall, according to the rules, alerted the opponents that I had just made a transfer to four clubs. I swear I did not close my eyes, look up in utter horror, or begin to sweat noticeably. I was too worried about how I was going to convince the Master that I really had diamonds and that three notrump was one huge super air ball. Suddenly, lo and behold, the Master announced to the whole table, "Three notrump is supposed to show clubs, but I don't believe it. Pass!"

Well, I could have jumped across the table and kissed Marshall. He had actually figured out that I had forgotten his beloved convention. What a player! As the play started I realized that something had gone awry. There were twelve sure tricks in notrump with the diamonds behaving. We had missed a cold slam.

"Marshall," I said, "the least you can do is honor my transfer bids. What do you think — I don't know what I am doing?"

I can't begin to describe the look Marshall gave me, and here I am, the only person in the world other than the Master who knows how to respond to two notrump properly.

Another Record

I remember reading somewhere that a declarer once made a small slam in spades with this combined trump holding:

NORTH *(dummy)*
♠ K 4 3

WEST
♠ A 9 8

EAST
♠ Q J

SOUTH *(declarer)*
♠ 10 9 6 5 2

It seems that after the opening lead, declarer laid down a side-suit ace, as if it were a singleton, and then led a low spade towards dummy where the king-queen of the side suit resided. West, fearing discards were coming, ran up with the ace of spades thus limiting his side to one trump trick with a combined holding of AQJ98. I must say, I was impressed with the defense — after all, it is not easy to take only one trick with that combined trump holding. However, time passed, and while I was playing with Paul Soloway, the following deal arose:

Vul: Neither
Dealer: North

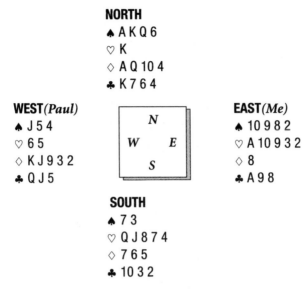

NORTH
♠ A K Q 6
♡ K
♢ A Q 10 4
♣ K 7 6 4

WEST (Paul)
♠ J 5 4
♡ 6 5
♢ K J 9 3 2
♣ Q J 5

EAST (Me)
♠ 10 9 8 2
♡ A 10 9 3 2
♢ 8
♣ A 9 8

SOUTH
♠ 7 3
♡ Q J 8 7 4
♢ 7 6 5
♣ 10 3 2

North opened two diamonds showing a strong three-suited hand. South responded two hearts announcing he would like to play hearts if that happened to be one of North's suits. No luck. North rebid two spades showing a singleton heart. Not wishing to strap his partner into playing a 4-2 fit, South 'rescued' to three clubs. North, reading the situation perfectly, raised to four clubs. South, showing great imagination, passed and the obvious contract was reached.

Paul made the 'normal' lead of the five of clubs! Dummy played low, and having perceived the position with my usual astuteness, I played the eight which lost to the ten.

At Trick 2 a heart was led to the king and the ace. Can you see it coming? Of course you can. I played the ace and a club. No book can describe the look that passed between Paul and me as his club honors came tumbling down. Of course four clubs was such a gruesome contract that we beat it one trick in spite of ourselves. Paul, once he regained his composure, even managed to pay me a compliment of sorts.

"Edwin," he said, "it was not easy to figure out a way that our side could take only one trump trick with a combined holding of AQJ985, but you managed it beautifully."

Fool, didn't he realize that history was in the making? I (we) may have set a record for futility that will last for years.

Addendum

Not long after the above hand was first published, a letter came my way indicating that although I should be proud of my accomplishments, I really was a piker compared to Don Caton and his partner, Mike Passell, who were defending one notrump with this combined spade holding:

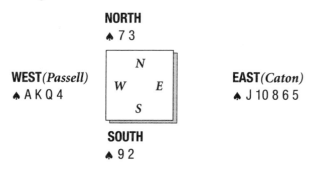

NORTH
♠ 7 3

WEST(*Passell*)
♠ A K Q 4

EAST(*Caton*)
♠ J 10 8 6 5

SOUTH
♠ 9 2

It seems that South had opened the bidding one of a suit and had rebid one notrump over partner's response. East-West, with their magnificent spade fit, had remained silent. West led the king of spades and East (fearing that South had ♠Qx) played the jack to deny the queen and to dissuade partner from underleading in case his original holding was ♠AKxx.

When West saw the jack, he thought that East had started with ♠J10x and rather than block the suit, he continued with a *low* spade. When East saw the low spade, he thought that partner's original spade holding was ♠KQ94 and rather than block the suit (East had an outside entry) played low assuming declarer would win with the now blank ace. The end result was the that South scored a trick with the doubleton nine of spades and the opponents with a combined holding of AKQJ108654 were unable to prevent the declarer from taking a trick in this suit in a notrump contract.

As much as I hate to admit it, I think these guys have got Paul and me beat.

Is This Game for Real?

◆

I collect bridge hands. I even file them away under various titles in an old shoe box. Who knows? Some day they may come in handy. Under the letter 'J' I file hands that I entitle 'joke hands'. They really happened all right, and they struck my funny bone somewhere, and besides, I didn't know where else to put them. Here's one from a National Mixed Pairs; the lineup was: South, adoring husband; North, beaming wife; East, Nervous Nellie (my partner); West, me.

Vul: North-South   **Dealer:** East

NORTH *(Beaming Wife)*
- ♠ A Q 9 7 5
- ♡ K 7
- ◇ 10 8 6 5 4
- ♣ 3

WEST *(Me)*
- ♠ 10 3
- ♡ 8 6 5
- ◇ A K J 9 7 3
- ♣ Q 10

EAST *(Nervous Nellie)*
- ♠ K 8 6 4
- ♡ A 3
- ◇ Q
- ♣ K J 9 7 6 2

SOUTH *(Adoring Husband)*
- ♠ J 2
- ♡ Q J 10 9 4 2
- ◇ 2
- ♣ A 8 5 4

WEST	NORTH	EAST	SOUTH
		1♣	1♡
2◇	2♠	dbl	3♡
dbl	all pass		

First, let me explain that my partner had never made a penalty double in the past unless they were down at least three. I, on the other hand, never double unless they can make an overtrick. I led the king of diamonds, and first dummy put down her trumps. Next came South's monologue: "Darling, you have the king of trumps! Thank you." Then came the spades, "Oh sweetheart, the ace of spades! How nice." Rather than show her diamonds, Beaming Wife put down her singleton club next. "Oh, you're kidding!" gushed South. "Not a singleton club too!" Now North was definitely afraid to put down her diamonds but, sensing her fear, South said, "Don't worry, honey, I don't have many of those,"

By this time I was wondering why they weren't in a slam, and my partner would have been happy to concede two overtricks just to get out of there. Trying to retain my composure, I shifted to a trump at Trick 2. My partner grabbed dummy's king and returned a trump. Declarer drew one more round of trumps and led the jack of spades. I played the ten, but to no avail. My partner was just too happy to take a trick, any trick, and she won the king.

My record was intact — my double had netted declarer an overtrick. My partner's record of never making the right play was also intact, and so we left for the next table (if she ducks the spade we actually beat the hand).

And now a true story of two friends of some years. Initials are going to be used to protect both parties. The story begins in Los Angeles some twenty years ago at the Los Angeles Bridge Club. BK and AB were rubber bridge partners and had sixty on. Both sides were vulnerable and this was the first of the two infamous hands:

WEST (BK)		EAST(AB)
♠ A 10 6 5 4	N	♠ Q 3
♡ A Q 10 4	W E	♡ K J 3
◇ A K	S	◇ J 6 5
♣ J 3		♣ A Q 8 7 2

BK	AB
1♠	2♣
3♡	4♡
4NT	5◇
5NT	6◇
6♡	pass

With the spade loser and the king of clubs offside, to go along with some bad breaks in the red suits, the hand was defeated two tricks. West was furious that East raised to four hearts, even though he himself had jumped to three hearts 'over score' (many play that a jump shift over score is forcing to what would be game with no partscore.) East-West still had that cursed sixty partial, and now came the next hand:

WEST (BK)
♠ K J 6 4
♡ K Q 10 9 8 2
◇ A
♣ K 3

EAST(AB)
♠ A Q 2
♡ 5 4 3
◇ 7 6
♣ A Q 8 6 2

BK	AB
1♡	2♣
2♡	pass

A diamond was led and when West saw the dummy he was livid. Sure that the partnership had missed a slam, he threw his cards face up on the table hurling insults left and right. First he accused AB of making a lousy four hearts slam try on the first hand, and now he said that AB had dogged the bidding on this one.

At this point North interjected saying that a cold slam had not been missed, and flashed the ace-jack-small of hearts. Still the torrent from West continued. Some of it was even directed at the owner of the club, who wasn't even in the game. That night BK's account was settled and he was barred from the club. BK and AB ceased to speak to one another.

Two years later BK and his family moved to Australia for seven years and then on to England where they live now. Twelve years pass since the incident and one day AB walks into the bridge club and is given a telephone number to call. He calls. He hears BK's voice on the other end. BK says, "I have decided to forgive you for making that slam try in hearts," — these, his first words after twelve years of silence.

The friendship was renewed and AB and BK had dinner with BK's family and they even had a social bridge game afterwards. Why do I feel like I have just written an article for the *National Enquirer*?

We will now end up with one of my favorites, although it took me two weeks to recover from the trauma. This was played at rubber bridge, with North-South vulnerable and forty on:

Vul: North-South
Dealer: East

```
                  NORTH
                  ♠ A Q 5
                  ♡ A K 10 2
                  ◇ 3
                  ♣ K J 9 6 5

WEST (Irving)        N          EAST (Me)
♠ 8 7 6 3 2                     ♠ K J 10 4
♡ J 8 4         W       E       ♡ 5
◇ 10 5 2                        ◇ A K 4
♣ 10 3              S           ♣ A Q 8 7 4

                  SOUTH
                  ♠ 9
                  ♡ Q 9 7 6 3
                  ◇ Q J 9 8 7 6
                  ♣ 2
```

WEST	NORTH	EAST	SOUTH
		1♣	pass
pass	dbl	redbl	4◇ !
all pass			

I was East, and afraid to double four diamonds for fear my partner might bid four hearts. West led the ten of clubs, and down came the dummy. South was furious. The nerve of his partner doubling one club with a singleton diamond! On and on South ranted. Finally he subsided and apologized, asking us not to pay any attention to his comments. (This, of course, is like hitting a man over the head with a sledgehammer and telling him to overlook the pain.)

Anyway, I won the queen of clubs and decided to base my defense on the hope that my partner had either J-x or 10-x-x of trumps, in which case constant club plays would build up the setting trick for us in the trump suit. I returned the seven of clubs at Trick 2, and declarer discarded a heart, winning the club in dummy with the nine. A diamond was led from dummy. I took the ace and my partner discarded the four of hearts. I said, "Irving!" — his name was Irving — "No diamonds?" Irving admitted to having a diamond and the four of hearts became a penalty card.

Clearly, it would do me no good to return a club at this point, because my partner would have to play that four of hearts anyway. Another brilliancy struck: I decided to return my singleton heart. Now, when I got in with my king of trumps, I could give my partner his overruff and in turn ruff a heart myself. I led my five of hearts. Declarer played low and my partner played the eight. Another exposed card! He had forgotten that he had to play the four which was lying on the table. Declarer now came back to his hand via a spade ruff, knocked out my other high diamond, and made his contract. I never did give Irving that club overruff.

Two weeks later Irving came up to tell me that it was actually all my fault. He had gone home that night and thought about what was going on in his mind at the time of the debacle. It turned out that when I played my ace of diamonds the first time the suit was led, Irving automatically placed declarer with the king. Irving knew I was going to return a club, and he thought that declarer would ruff high with his probable K-Q-J of trumps, and that he (Irving)would discard a heart — which he did. If I had won the first diamond with the king, he would not have been one trick ahead of himself, and so I was to blame after all. Of course.

PART SIX

High-level Bridge

God Save Our Country

The phone rang. "Hamman speaking."

"Yes, Robert, what can I do for you?"

"First, I want to apologize for all the nasty things I've ever said about those exotic bidding sequences that you and Marshall use, and second, I want you to play a hand for me."

The man who was soon to represent our country in Italy in the World Championships then called off the following hand which took place at the office in Los Angeles. (The 'office' is the L.A. Bridge Club, so termed in order to add a little respectability to our wayward lives.)

"So, how do you play this hand with a low diamond out?"

NORTH
♠ A 10 9 x x
♡ 10 x x
♢ x
♣ A J x x

```
      N
  W       E
      S
```

SOUTH
♠ Q J x x x
♡ J x x
♢ x x x
♣ x x

"Just a minute," I said. "What's the contract?"

"Guess," said Bob.

"Four spades?"

"No."

"Six spades?"

"No."

"Five spades?"

"No."

"*Clubs*?"

"No."

"Four hearts?"

"No."

"Three notrump?"

"You're getting warmer."

I just couldn't stand it any longer, and exploded, "Please, Bob, just tell me the contract!"

"*Three diamonds doubled, what else?*" Bob roared.

"You must be joking," I gasped. "Was this for money?"

"Yes."

"Your own money?"

"Sure, my own money"

"Who were you?"

"North."

"And who was South?"

"Paul Soloway."

"How'd the bidding go?"

"Very logically."

Vul: Neither

WEST	NORTH	EAST	SOUTH
		1◇	pass
1♡	2NT[1]	pass	pass[2]
dbl	3♣[3]	pass	pass[4]
dbl	pass	pass	3◇[5]
dbl	pass[6]	pass	pass

The bidding as explained by Hamman:

1. My two notrump bids are for the other two suits when the opponents have bid two suits.
2. Soloway plays the two notrump overcall for the minors even if one of the minor suits has been bid.
3. Two notrump doubled did not appeal to me.
4. If we get doubled I'll run to my longer minor. I hope Hamman isn't worried about me interpreting his two notrump overcall. After all, I've been around.
5. Might as well play in our longest suit.
6. Might as well — he must have at least seven diamonds.

"So what finally happened?" I asked, not in the mood to play three diamonds doubled on these cards.

"The story has a happy ending," Bob said. "The opponents could have beaten us eight, but they beat us only seven. They slopped a trick."

"Forgive my asking, but are you really going to Italy?"

"Sure — you know I am."

"God save our country!"

Key Cards

◆

Playing with P.O. (Per Olov) Sundelin, the Swedish star, in the Blue Ribbon Pairs, our 'experienced' partnership had the following to contend with:

WEST *(Me)*		EAST *(P.O.)*
♠ A J 3	*N*	♠ K 10 5
♡ K 9 4 2	*W E*	♡ A Q J 8 5
◇ A J 7 6	*S*	◇ K 10 9 8
♣ A 5		♣ 3

As dealer, I opened one notrump and P.O. responded two clubs, which was doubled. I bid two hearts and P.O. countered with four clubs. Having discussed our methods for roughly fifteen minutes prior to game time, I decided this was Gerber. P.O. said later he was prepared to have me think it was either a Gerber, a splinter, or a cue-bid. As we had decided to play Roman Key Card Blackwood, I responded four hearts showing one or four key cards. I hoped this wouldn't sound like a sign-off.

P.O. thought I had poor trumps and was signing off. He now bid four notrump. Well, I thought, I've already shown four key cards but what the hell, I'll show four more. I responded five diamonds, once again showing one or four key cards. He now signed off in five hearts, thinking I had one ace. Having already shown eight key cards I was not about to play in less than a slam. I concluded the highly scientific auction with six hearts.

Now to the play.

I won the club lead, drew trumps in two rounds, and ruffed a club in dummy. I continued with the ace and jack of diamonds. When North played low I rose with the king, catching air, and exited with a diamond. The opponents had to lead a spade (or give me a ruff and a sluff) and I made six hearts.

Later it was pointed out that I had misplayed the slam — at matchpoints I should finesse the diamond, giving myself the best chance to make seven. Even if the finesse loses, but my opponent has the doubleton queen of diamonds, he will be endplayed. Furthermore, if North had started with queen-fourth of diamonds, I would still have had to guess the spade queen after playing ace-king of diamonds in my line.

My excuse was that I was so exhausted after having shown eight key cards that I could not be expected to find the best line of play.

Me in the World Championships*!

$\diamond$

It has gone virtually unnoticed until now because of all the attention paid to the cheating scandal in Bermuda, but early in the week of the championship I found myself playing one sixteen-board session against the great Benito Garozzo and Giorgio Belladonna. Yeah, me, Walter Bingham, non-expert. This is how it happened.

The US team and its followers were gathered in the suite of Freddie Sheinwold, the captain, after the first afternoon session against the Italians. From four floors up the sunlight was sparkling on the blue Atlantic Ocean. The players were comparing results and rehashing hands while the rest of us stood around nibbling on the cold cuts Paula Sheinwold had provided. Toward the end of the break, Sheinwold announced that in the second session it would be Bob Hamman and Bob Wolff in the Open Room, Billy Eisenberg and Eddie Kantar in the Closed. Paul Soloway and John Swanson, he said, would have the rest of the afternoon off. Whereupon Nina Swanson said swell, maybe John and Paul would finally take her into Hamilton to shop for sweaters. The way she said it, it sounded more like an order, and off they went. As a member of the press, I was entitled to sit in the Closed Room, so when Eisenberg and Kantar departed, I went with them. As we passed Billy's room, he said he had to make a quick stop and would meet us downstairs.

Eddie and I went to the elevators, pushed the 'down' button and waited. And waited. And waited. I must explain that although the Southampton Princess was in many ways a splendid hotel, its eleva-

---

* The first part of this article was written by Walter Bingham, of *Sports Illustrated*. He was covering the World Bridge Championships for the magazine as he has often done in the past.

tors were weird. Mostly they never came. When they did and you got in, the doors would remain open for what seemed like hours. Finally, when those doors decided that it was time to close, nothing could stop them, including late-arriving human bodies.

In this case, two strange things happened. The red light for one of the elevators went on, but the doors never opened and eventually the light went off. When we were able to get on one and had pushed the button for the first floor, we sailed right past it, down to the lower lobby. Getting off, we decided it would be more prudent to walk back up.

Garozzo and Belladonna were waiting, along with two monitors to work the bidding screens, a couple of solemn officials of the World Bridge Federation, and a busboy with a tray full of Cokes. Benito and Giorgio were seated East and West. Eddie took the North chair. South was for Billy, but Billy had not yet arrived. I drew up a chair behind Eddie. Maury Braunstein, the tournament director, brought in four boards. We were set, ready for play. But no Billy.

When five minutes had passed and Billy had still not appeared, he was officially late. A phone call to his room produced no answer. The Federation officials were huddled with Maury Braunstein, trying to decide what to do, when Susan Gunther, the tournament chairman, burst into the room to say that one of the hotel elevators was stuck between the second and third floors. Mechanics had estimated it would take two hours to release the passengers, one of whom was presumably Billy.

In instances where a player is tardy for world championship play, the rules are clear — the third pair may be substituted. Except that in this case the third pair was somewhere in Hamilton trying on Shetlands. With Swanson and Soloway unavailable, the Italians could, if they wanted, claim a forfeit — and who could blame them if they did, since not long before the US had accused one of their pairs of cheating?

By this time Sandro Salvetti, the Italian captain, was in the room, huddled with Garozzo and Belladonna. Freddie Sheinwold had also appeared. After five minutes the Italians turned to the rest of us in the room and announced their decision. They would not accept a forfeit. Instead they would allow Sheinwold and Kantar to select any partner of their choice, provided that player had no master points to his credit. None. Zero. That ruled out Captain Sheinwold. It ruled out Ozzie Jacoby who was roaming the lobby in his bathing suit. It also ruled out Edgar Kaplan, who might have enjoyed a moment away from the commentator's table. Lew Mathe, just itching for some action, and Dick Frey. It even ruled out Nina, if she had been there. But not me. I was the only person who could tell a heart from a diamond (barely) who did not have a suitcase full of points, red ones, gold ones, whatever. Sheinwold had no choice. He looked at me, shrugged, pointed to the South seat, and the game was on.

(Kantar speaking now.)

I had better take over from Walter to describe this session of sixteen boards. As there was not time to discuss conventions, coupled with the fact that Walter doesn't play any besides Blackwood and Stayman, I figured we had a small survival quotient (bigger than if he had played any, however, since the confusion factor was no longer present). Besides, I hadn't played strong two-bids, grandiose jump overcalls, and cuebids showing first-round controls for years. Maybe something good would happen — by mistake.

I wished I had some way to calm Walter down, as he was obviously nervous. Shaking is actually the proper term. In an earlier session my partner, Billy Eisenberg, had tried to calm me down by lighting up (unfortunately, he lit up a gum wrapper by mistake). I neither smoke nor chew so we were in big trouble. Fortunately for us the first few hands were rather cut and dried, which means Walter didn't have to be the declarer. Our defense wasn't exactly first-rate, which means that while we didn't revoke, I could see the World Championship being likely to vanish in overtricks alone if something good didn't happen soon.

Walter was also aware that we weren't taking all of our tricks on defense, and that was adding to his general discomfort. On Board 6 we once again found ourselves on defense. Ugh.

(Directions rearranged for reader convenience.)

NORTH *(Belladonna)*
♠ 9 7 5 3 2
♡ K J 7 6
◊ 10 9 4
♣ 3

WEST *(Me)*
♠ A J 10 8 4
♡ 9 8 2
◊ J
♣ A K Q 9

EAST *(Bingham)*
♠ K Q
♡ A Q 5 4 3
◊ 7 2
♣ 10 8 7 6

SOUTH *(Garozzo)*
♠ 6
♡ 10
◊ A K Q 8 6 5 3
♣ J 5 4 2

WEST	NORTH	EAST	SOUTH
		1♡	4◊
4♡	5◊	pass	pass
dbl	all pass		

Opening Lead: ♣K

Belladonna had a real problem over 4♡. Should he let Bingham play a hand when trumps weren't breaking or should he let Bingham and me defend? He had seen our act before so he bid. Walter was happy to pass 5♡ with his 2½ honor tricks (I forgot to tell you he still counts that way) and I felt reasonably secure in doubling even though I too had seen our act before. After all, Walter had opened the bidding and they were vulnerable. What was going on here?

At Trick 2 I hastily shifted to a trump and Bingham nodded, presumably understanding that I was trying to stop club ruffs in dummy. Garozzo immediately led the ten of hearts and ducked it. Walter, in his haste to play a second trump, won the ten with the ace. Benito naturally placed me with Q-x-x of hearts. He won the trump return in dummy, played the king of hearts discarding a spade, and ruffed a heart. Alas, no queen from me and Garozzo had to go down two, taking eight diamonds and a heart. Plus 500 for us. We finally had a good result.

It did not go unnoticed that, if Walter had won the ten with the queen, Garozzo would later have run the king of hearts through Walter, setting up the jack and seven for two discards once the 9-8 both fell. Looks crossed the table. Naturally Walter was apologizing all over the place for 'wasting' his ace on declarer's ten as play resumed.

A few more hands, a few more overtricks down the tubes, and then Board 9 which caused a bit of a furor.

Vul: North-South
Dealer: West

NORTH *(Me)*
♠ 4 3
♡ Q 10 8 4
♢ A 5 4
♣ A J 8 3

WEST *(Garozzo)*
♠ K Q
♡ 9 2
♢ K J 10 9 8
♣ K Q 7 5

EAST *(Belladonna)*
♠ 5 2
♡ A J 6 3
♢ 7 3 2
♣ 10 9 6 4

SOUTH *(Bingham)*
♠ A J 10 9 8 7 6
♡ K 7 5
♢ Q 6
♣ 2

WEST	NORTH	EAST	SOUTH
1♢	pass	1♡	4♠!
all pass			

Opening Lead: ♠K

It might be pointed out here that Walter's main bridge experience has been on commuter trains to New York each morning. In these games Walter is the big cheese. Consequently, he bids quite a bit, as he usually winds up making his contracts against inferior defense.

Meanwhile back at the table, Benito elected to lead the king of spades, probably thinking that Bingham must have about ten spades and that the chances of his making two defensive tricks in that suit were close to nil. Bingham won the ace and exited with the jack, hardly noticing the three or four tricks my dummy had provided for him — vulnerable yet!

Garozzo was in trouble — leading either red suit immediately gives up a trick, and the king of clubs is surely best. Garozzo exited with the even more tricky queen of clubs. Bingham, by now, had an advanced case of the jitters. In fact, I sure that all his cards would soon be spilling on to the table. Besides, he always wanted to grab cards from the dummy instead of calling them.

"Eight of clubs," he finally said. I looked up and played the eight. Bingham was horror-struck.

"I meant the ace, I meant the ace!" he screamed maniacally.

Garozzo and Belladonna looked at each other and then at Bingham pityingly. They didn't want to take advantage, but the director who happened to be in the room at the time ruled that the eight of clubs was a played card.

This time Garozzo was in worse shape than before. If he played another club there was no telling which club Bingham would play, but it might be the jack. A diamond might not be safe if Bingham had the queen, and the heart suit looked decidedly unappetizing. In the end, Garozzo exited with the king of diamonds.

Bingham looked up. He smiled. He won the ace of diamonds, discarded a heart on the ace of clubs and said very carefully, "I concede a heart — making four spades, vulnerable."

Play resumed. They bid a cold slam, but we naturally let them make seven. They bid a cold game in spades, making six (we were doing better — I led an ace, but we still got squeezed), and finally they stopped in two clubs and we held them to five holding four sure tricks. Nevertheless, the match was definitely not out of hand. Between Walter's brilliancies and the overtricks, things were almost even going into last hand.

Vul: North-South
Dealer: South

NORTH *(Me)*
♠ A Q
♡ Q J 10 4
◇ K 4 3 2
♣ A K 5

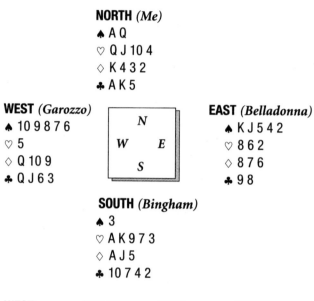

WEST *(Garozzo)*
♠ 10 9 8 7 6
♡ 5
◇ Q 10 9
♣ Q J 6 3

EAST *(Belladonna)*
♠ K J 5 4 2
♡ 8 6 2
◇ 8 7 6
♣ 9 8

SOUTH *(Bingham)*
♠ 3
♡ A K 9 7 3
◇ A J 5
♣ 10 7 4 2

WEST	NORTH	EAST	SOUTH
			1♡
pass	4NT	pass	5♡
pass	5NT	pass	6◇
pass	6♡	all pass	

Even if Walter had both missing kings I wasn't sure I was going to plop him down in seven. The pressure of a vulnerable World Championship grand slam might just be a little too much for him to handle at this point.

In any case, 6♡ was the right contract and the ten of spades was led. Walter had no trouble playing the ace as nobody on the commuter trains underleads kings — ever. But just to see who had it, Walter played the queen of spades at Trick 2 and beamed as

Belladonna put up the king which was ruffed. I smiled encouragingly. After all, so far nothing too terrible had happened.

There was an eerie sort or of silence at the table as everyone knew that whatever line of play Walter chose, it was unlikely to be duplicated in the other room. Walter's next move was to play three rounds of hearts leaving the highest heart in dummy. Garozzo, with little choice, parted with two spades.

Now Walter attacked diamonds. He led a diamond to the king, Garozzo playing the ten. Walter eyed that card suspiciously. Could it a be a singleton? Perhaps Q-10 doubleton? Obviously it wasn't a singleton or else Garozzo would have started with two red singletons, so it must be Q-10 doubleton! Walter placed a diamond to the ace triumphantly. The nine fell. He looked at me. I looked at him. What the hell did he want from me? I was only the dummy.

Walter exited with the jack of diamonds to Garozzo's queen. Benito quickly played the jack of clubs to dummy's ace and Belladonna's eight. Walter looked at me again. What was it this time, I wondered? Didn't he know the four of diamonds was high? Why did I bid so damn much? I'll be an old man before this hand is over, I thought. Finally Walter ruffed and was shattered when Garozzo discarded yet another spade.

"I'm sorry," he muttered, "I just couldn't remember," Silence. Walter turned his attention to the club suit. He remembered earlier that Benito had led a queen from the king-queen and this time he had led the jack. Perhaps he had the queen as well. But what about that distressing eight Belladonna had played? Never mind about the eight. Belladonna was trying to fool him. Nobody fools Bingham, he thought as he crunched the ten of clubs on the table. Garozzo played low unhesitatingly.

"Small club," cried Walter.

Wonder of wonder, the ten of clubs held, Belladonna's nine came tumbling down and the small slam was made — vulnerable. What is more quiet than absolute silence?

As soon as we left the room I started pounding Walter on the back. "Great game," I said. "Let's compare."

We met Sheinwold, Hamman, Wolff, and a bedraggled Eisenberg

in Room 416 to compare. Four boards were actually pushes. On nine boards we lost small swings, almost always due to letting them make overtricks or not making enough tricks when we played the hand. But those nine boards only accounted for 25 IMPs.

On Board 6 where Bingham took the ace of hearts rather than the queen we picked up 7 IMPs because five diamonds doubled went down only one trick in the other room with Hamman declaring. On Board 9 the Italians didn't reach game, stopping in three spades, also making four, so we picked up another 10 IMPs. And finally on Board 16 the Italian declarer took the diamond finesse and could no longer make six hearts so we picked up a fat 17 IMPs. We actually won 9 IMPs for the session.

Walter was besieged with warm handshakes. Soloway and Swanson returned from their buying trip with Nina and could hardly believe their ears. Bingham was the hero of the hour. Then a knock on the door. It was a message from the Italian Captain. It simply said, "*Por favor,* no more Bingham! Sincerely, Sandro Salvetti."

After that, you know the story. The Italians, not having to contend with our secret weapon, went on to win the World Championship again, but had they let us use the 'commuter cannon' for just one more session…

PS. For any reader who hasn't figured it out yet, this entire story is fictional.

The System in Action

$\diamond$

One of the main difficulties in playing so many conventions is that it puts an added mental strain on the partnership. Not only do you have to remember what you are playing, but you also have to remember the ramifications and minor changes you have adopted to fit your own bidding style.

Fortunately, Marshall Miles, my most frequent partner, and I seldom forget what we are playing. On a good day, we never have more than three mental lapses a session. One 'minor' misunderstanding stands out. Playing in the Nationals at Lexington, Kentucky, we arrived at a contract of seven clubs, with A-K-8 of clubs facing a void!

As no book that either Marshall or I have ever read described the proper play (for no losers) with this trump combination, our contract was not successful. Since many players in Lexington were interested in exactly how we managed to get to this contract, I thought I would outline the bidding, and point out all the advanced nuances known only to those select few who can arrive logically at this type of contract.

Three meanings will be attached to each bid:

1) *The systemic meaning:* what the bid is supposed to mean.
2) *The bidder's meaning:* what the bidder thought the bid was supposed to mean.
3) *The interpretation:* what the bidder's partner thought the bid meant.

Theoretically, in a good partnership, these three meanings should be one and the same. However, there have been times when there has been a slight difference of opinion even in the best partnerships.

Now for the hand. Marshall was West and dealer; I was East.

WEST *(Marshall)*		EAST *(Me)*
♠ K J 8 7 6	N	♠ A Q 5 4
♡ A K 3	W E	♡ 5 4
◇ A 4	S	◇ Q 10 8 7 6 5 3
♣ A K 8		♣ —

THE BIDDING: ROUND 1

West: Two clubs

Systemic meaning: a strong hand (artificial bid).

Bidder's meaning: I have a strong hand.

Interpretation: all right, you have a strong hand.

East: Two Diamonds.

Systemic meaning: a weak hand, or one that cannot be accurately limited (artificial response).

Bidder's meaning: I know I'm supposed to have a weak hand but I really don't know what to respond, so I'll bide my time.

Interpretation: probably a weak hand (notice how well we understand each other!).

ROUND 2

West: Two notrump.

Systemic meaning: a balanced hand with 22-24 points.

Bidder's meaning: same.

Interpretation: same.

East: Four diamonds.

Systemic meaning: a specialized conventional bid asking opener to show a four-card minor if he has one.

Bidder's meaning: I should have bid three diamonds in the first place, so now I have to show my strength. I'll worry about my spades later.

Interpretation: good — we have a chance to use our new convention! I hope he hasn't forgotten and I hope he realizes that I haven't forgotten! He wants to know if I have a four-card minor.

ROUND 3

West: Four hearts.

Systemic meaning: a conventional response showing no four-card minor.

Bidder's meaning: I have no four-card minor. This convention sure is working smoothly! (Why does he look so serious? Is he worrying that I've forgotten our understanding? I remember, I remember!)

Interpretation: wonderful! He fits my diamond suit and is showing me a heart control. Looks like we are heading for a grand slam that the rest of the field may miss. (We got there, all right!)

East: Four spades.

Systemic meaning: from here on in the system gets a little foggy as we never had a chance to use our four diamond minor-suit asking bid before.

Bidder's meaning: I think I'll show my ace of spades, and if it turns out that we have a spade fit, I can always say that I bid my spades. Sort of a two-way bid.

Interpretation: he asked for my four-card minor and I gave him a denial when I bid four hearts. He didn't bid either minor or sign off at four notrump, so he must be cuebidding the ace or a void in spades. He must be terribly long in the minors and, with that master cuebid he just made, I can't let this hand play in less than seven. I must have all the right cards. I might shake him up a bit with my next bid, but what else can I do?

ROUND 4

West: Seven clubs

Systemic meaning: a hand that should play in seven clubs.

Bidder's meaning: it's so nice to play with a partner who describes his hand so well! Wait till I tell them back home about this one. I can just see my partner's hand:

$$\spadesuit — \quad \heartsuit xx \quad \diamondsuit KQxxx \quad \clubsuit QJ10xxx$$

(Please notice how clearly Marshall gauged my heart holding.)

Interpretation: why, that sneaky devil! So it was a solid club suit all along. No need to worry, Marshall old boy — I got the word; I'm not going to pull it. Of course you don't know that I am void in clubs but your suit is certainly solid. I guess we must be in our best spot. (I just hope the clubs break.)

PS. For those of you who are still there, the clubs did break! With the lucky 6-4 trump break, Marshall went down only five tricks. He later told me that good defense could have beaten him six, but he had played the hand very deceptively. He also said that the opponents could not understand our bidding. (I had left the table after they took their third trick.) He also told me, gleefully, that they had let him make his eight of clubs by playing a fourth round of hearts. I nodded admiringly.

Other bridge titles from Master Point Press

Partnership Bidding   *A workbook* by Mary Paul
0-9698461-0-X   96 pp. PB   Can $ 9.95   US$7.95   UK£5.99

"A wonderfully useful book." *BRIDGE magazine*

There Must Be A Way... *52 challenging bridge hands*
by Andrew Diosy (foreword by Eddie Kantar)
0-9698461-1-8   96 pp. PB   US & Canada $ 9.95   UK£6.99

You Have to See This   *52 more challenging bridge problems*
by Andrew Diosy and Linda Lee
0-9698461-9-3   96 pp PB   Can $12.95   US$ 9.95   UK£7.99

"A frustratingly enjoyable read." *ACBL Bulletin*
"Treat yourself to a gem of a book." *Eddie Kantar*

Tales out of School   *'Bridge 101' and other stories*
by David Silver (foreword by Dorothy Hayden Truscott)
0-9698461-2-6   128 pp PB   Can $ 12.95   US$9.95   UK£6.99

A Study in Silver   *A second collection of bridge stories* by David Silver
0-9698461-5-0   128 pp PB   Can $ 12.95   US$ 9.95   UK£6.99

"Every bridge book by Silver has a golden lining." *The Toronto Star*
"Hilarious." *Alan Truscott, New York Times*

Focus On Declarer Play by Danny Roth
0-9698461-3-4   128 pp PB   Can $ 12.95   US $9.95   UK£6.99

Focus On Defence by Danny Roth
0-9698461-4-2   128 pp PB   Can $ 12.95   US $9.95   UK£6.99

Focus on Bidding by Danny Roth
1-894154-06-1   160 pp PB   Can. $14.95   US$ 11.95   UK£7.99

"Far and away Danny Roth's best work so far... Highly recommended for anyone
between bright novice and experienced tournament player."
Bridge Plus magazine.

The Complete Book of BOLS Bridge Tips edited by Sally Brock
0-9698461-6-9   176 pp PB, photographs   Can $ 24.95 US$17.95

"The quality of each and every tip is exceptional and we maintain that the book cannot fail to improve your bridge." *Australian Bridge*

The Bridge Player's Bedside Book edited by Tony Forrester
0-9698461-8-5   256pp HC   Can $27.95   US$ 19.95

"A delightful collection." *Matthew Granovetter, Jerusalem Post*

Easier Done Than Said *Brilliancy at the bridge table* by P.K. Paranjape
1-894154-00-2   128pp PB   Can $15.95 US$ 12.95 UK£9.99

"An outstanding book." *ACBL Bulletin*

Bridge, Zia... and me
by Michael Rosenberg (foreword by Zia Mahmood)
1-894154-04-5   192pp PB   Can $19.95 US$ 15.95

"Michael has the most fascinating mind for bridge you will ever encounter." *Zia Mahmood*

World Class *Conversations with the bridge masters* by Marc Smith
1-894154-15-0   272 pp PB   Can. $24.95 US$ 17.95 UK£12.99

Two dozen of the world's best players share their thoughts and ideas on their own careers and on the game of bridge. **October 1999.**

Murder at the Bridge Table   by Matthew Granovetter
1-894154-11-8   304 pp PB   Can. $19.95 US$ 14.95 UK£10.99

Improve your duplicate game as you solve a murder mystery!
"Mozart's opera is an enduring masterpiece, and so, too, may be 'Murder at the Bridge Table'" *Frank Stewart, ACBL Bulletin..*

I Shot My Bridge Partner   by Matthew Granovetter
1-894154-12-6   380 pp PB   Can. $19.95 US$ 14.95 UK£10.99

Improve your bridge game as you solve a murder mystery!
"Crazy, logical, instructive — but most of all it's screamingly, drop-dead funny" *Alfred Sheinwold.*

Around the World in 80 Hands   by Zia Mahmood
1-894154-08-8   256 pp PB   Can. $22.95 US$ 16.95 UK£11.99
One of the world's top players shares his favorite hands and bridge stories.

MASTER POINT PRESS

22 Lower Village Gate Toronto, Ontario M5P 3L7

(416) 932-9766   Internet: www.pathcom.com/~raylee/